MW00647391

INTRODUCTION TO LARGE LANGUAGE MODELS FOR BUSINESS LEADERS

RESPONSIBLE AI STRATEGY BEYOND FEAR AND HYPE

BYTE-SIZED LEARNING SERIES
BOOK 2

I. ALMEIDA

Copyright © 2024 by Now Next Later AI

All rights reserved.

No part of this book may be reproduced in any form or by any electronic or mechanical means, including information storage and retrieval systems, without written permission from the publisher, except for the use of brief quotations in a book review.

We are the most trusted and effective learning platform dedicated to empowering leaders with the knowledge and skills needed to harness the power of AI safely and ethically. Join now to enjoy free lessons and webinars.

CONTENTS

A BALANCED GUIDE TO LLMS AND GENERATIVE AI FOR BUSINESS

arge language models (LLMs) like GPT-4 and Claude 2 represent a technology with the potential for transforming business and society, if applied judiciously. This book provides leaders with a comprehensive yet accessible guide to using LLMs for competitive advantage today while laying ethical foundations for long-term positive impact.

LLMs leverage deep neural networks trained on vast text datasets to generate remarkably human-like language. Their capabilities in automated content creation, knowledge synthesis, and natural language interaction can enhance workflows across marketing, customer service, HR, R&D, legal, and more. However, hype and fear both risk distorting perspectives on LLMs. In this book, I aim to support nuanced understanding and prudent application.

I survey the rapid progress of LLMs, explain technical concepts in non-technical terms, provide business use cases, offer implementation strategies, explore impacts on the workforce, and discuss ethical considerations. The narrative arc aims not to celebrate blindly nor condemn prematurely, but to inform readers for thoughtful adoption, maximizing real-world benefits while proactively addressing risks. Wise business application demands avoiding reactionary hype and fear by grounding discussion in balanced technical and ethical insights.

LLMs represent the most impactful and commercially mature subtype of the broader field of generative AI. Generative AI refers to systems that can autonomously create content such as text, images, audio, or video. However, in this book, I focus specifically on language-based generative systems for several key reasons:

- Natural language interaction enables intuitive communication of complex concepts, allowing the book to ground technical discussion in accessible examples and narratives.

- LLMs currently exhibit the most advanced generative abilities because of the nuanced complexity of human language. Mastering language provides a foundation for other modalities.

- These models present the clearest adoption opportunities and risks for business in the near-term compared to other generative technologies still earlier in their development.

- Language provides a universal interface for human collaboration and knowledge sharing. LLMs' abilities to synthesize and generate textual

information have uniquely widespread
applications.

While not exhaustive on visual or audio generation, the reader will gain context on the broader generative AI field to make informed evaluations. However, language serves as the core thread connecting concepts and illustrating capabilities in an understandable frame. My focus on LLMs aims to balance comprehensiveness with coherence for accessible business guidance. Leaders will gain integrated perspectives essential to setting sound strategies amidst AI's rapid evolution and hype.

2

INTRODUCTION TO LLMS

Large language models have rapidly risen to prominence as one of the most promising and transformative technologies in artificial intelligence. Powered by advances in computational power and fueled by immense datasets, LLMs have evolved remarkably in just the last decade from simple statistical models to complex neural network architectures with capabilities rivaling or exceeding human language proficiency.

In this chapter, I will chronicle the development of LLMs, highlighting key innovations and milestones that have led to models like GPT-4 and Claude 2. By understanding where LLMs originated and how they have progressed, we gain insight into their potential, as well as pressing questions around their responsible development and deployment. This chapter will introduce and define some of the key concepts I will explore in more depth later in the book.

The Quest for Language AI

Long before the era of deep learning, researchers were interested in statistical language modeling—developing mathematical models that could predict likely sequences of words based on patterns in text. Early language models included n-gram models that looked at the probability of a word appearing given the previous n-1 words. Though limited to local statistical patterns, these models were successfully used in applications like spell check and word prediction.

In the late 2000s, a major shift happened in the way we understood and processed language with the help of computers. This progress came as neural language models, a type of advanced computer program inspired by the human brain. One of the standout models from this era was called Word2Vec[1].

Think of Word2Vec as a method that teaches computers to understand the relationship and context between words like how humans do. Instead of just reading words as isolated bits of information, Word2Vec processes large amounts of text to determine how words relate to one another. This process results in creating 'embeddings'.

Imagine if every word in a language was represented by a point on a map. Some points (or words) are closer to each other because they share similar meanings or are often used in the same context. These 'points' or representations are what we call embeddings. So, words like "king" and "queen" would be closer on this map because they both refer to royalty and are often mentioned together. What's fascinating is that Word2Vec can even capture more complex relationships and analogies between words based on these

embeddings. For instance, it can recognize that the relationship between "man" and "woman" is like the relationship
between "king" and "queen".

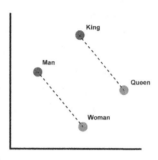

Word vector illustration.[68]

However, while Word2Vec was revolutionary, it had its limitations. The primary one being that when it was trying to
predict a word or its meaning, it only looked at the immediate words around it, much like only seeing the nearest
landmarks on a map. This means it didn't always consider
the larger context or the entire sentence, which sometimes
led to less accurate interpretations of language. Nonetheless, it was a giant leap in the quest to make computers
understand and generate human-like text.

The Rise of Transformers

The world of language processing witnessed a paradigm
shift in 2017, a revolutionary change brought by introducing
the "transformer" architecture. The term "transformer" in
this context isn't about shape-shifting robots, but it signifies
an advancement in how computers comprehend and
generate human-like text. This advancement has, over

recent years, underpinned some of the most significant strides in artificial intelligence.

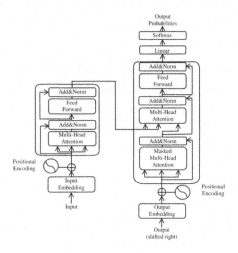

Transformer Model Architecture[65]

At the heart of the transformer architecture is a mechanism known as "self-attention". To understand the significance of self-attention, imagine reading a novel. As you traverse through the pages, you don't just focus on the immediate words you're reading. Instead, your brain constantly references previous sections, characters, or themes, allowing you to draw a meaningful connection between past and present details. This holistic approach to reading is akin to the self-attention mechanism, where the model doesn't merely focus on a word's immediate neighbors but considers the entire context, making associations between words that might be far apart.

Now, why was this so groundbreaking? Earlier models, like the aforementioned Word2Vec, were like tunnel-visioned readers, focusing primarily on neighboring words. The transformer architecture, on the other hand, treats a sentence or paragraph more holistically. Each word can "attend" to all other words, giving the model an unprecedented understanding of context.

The paper titled "Attention Is All You Need,"[2] published by researchers from Google, was the linchpin in this transformation. This paper didn't just introduce a theoretical concept; it provided a robust framework that could be implemented and scaled. The central idea was that, in many cases, focusing on the relationships (or attention) between different parts of an input was more crucial than the actual content or sequence of the input. The paper's title elegantly encapsulated this idea: attention mechanisms, particularly self-attention, were paramount to achieving high performance in many language tasks.

It's worth noting the sheer elegance and efficiency of transformers. While the concept might sound complex, transformers often require fewer computations than their predecessors for a given task. This is because, instead of sequentially processing information (word by word, or step by step), transformers can process all words or parts of a sentence in parallel. This parallel processing not only speeds up computations but also allows for a richer understanding of context.

GPT-1, released in 2017, was the first transformer-based LLM. It had 117 million parameters—think of parameters like the knobs and levers that control how the machine processes language data. The more parameters, the more nuanced patterns the model can learn by analyzing large amounts of text during training. Though tiny compared to modern LLM sizes, GPT-1's 117 million parameters learned enough complex language relationships to outperform substantially previous statistical models at tasks like answering questions and drawing inferences from passages.

This breakthrough confirmed the potential for even more advanced language understanding if these transformer models were scaled up and trained on more text data. Much as bigger data and faster computers enabled businesses to gain deeper market insights, more parameters and data powered LLMs enabled businesses to gain deeper comprehension of language. GPT-1 showed the promise of the transformer approach, motivating rapid growth in model capacity that continues today. Soon after, in 2018, Google introduced BERT (Bidirectional Encoder Representations from Transformers.)

GPT-2, released by OpenAI in 2019, benefited from 10x more parameters and 10x more data than GPT-1. Its impressive natural language generation capabilities showed the benefits of scale, though concerns about potential misuse led OpenAI to limit public access initially. Its 1.5 billion parameter version, however, was released fully in 2020.

GPT-3 took another leap in 2020, scaled up to 175 billion parameters trained on over a trillion words of filtered text data, including the Common Crawl dataset, a web-crawled dataset. It required computational resources on the order of thousands of PetaFLOP/s-days. PetaFLOP/s-days refers to measuring the total compute used to train a model by multiplying the number of PetaFLOP/s (a measure of computer processing speed) by the number of days of training. This imposed training costs exceeding millions of dollars, with environmental impacts that required optimization.

GPT-3 showed a remarkable capability called few-shot learning. What is few-shot learning? In simple terms, it means GPT-3 could successfully perform tasks like translation and question answering with just a few examples showing what to do. Show GPT-3 just a single translated sentence pair, and it could translate new sentences between those languages. Give it a couple of examples of question-answer pairs, and it could answer new questions on that topic. This ability to learn from just a few examples stunned researchers. Previous models required far more training examples to gain skills.

Few-shot learning opened up GPT-3's versatility for translation, question-answering, app development, robot control and more—all powered by simple natural language prompting. In business terms, it required less training data to gain new skills. This breakthrough revealed the possibilities of scale and fine-tuning transformer architectures, inspiring intense research interest in LLMs since 2020.

GPT-4 continues the trend of exponential growth, likely employing a mixture of expert models, together reaching the trillion-parameter scale and multi-trillion word training datasets. Problematically, details remain undisclosed, but it likely builds on GPT-3 foundations with more advanced training techniques. The steady march upwards in scale proves that language modeling continues to benefit tremendously from added data and compute.

Beyond OpenAI, other organizations like Google, Meta, Anthropic, Baidu, and more have trained LLMs at scale. Except for Meta, these businesses focus on delivering services via APIs rather than releasing full models. However, open source LLMs are beginning to show impressive results with 2023 releases, such as Dolly 2.0, LLaMA, Alpaca, and Vicuna.

Foundational Models

In 2021, researchers at the Stanford Institute for Human-Centered Artificial Intelligence (HAI) introduced the paradigm of foundation models[3] to describe influential AI models like LLMs that serve as a foundation for down-stream tasks. Foundation models are pre-trained on vast datasets, then fine-tuned on more specialized data to excel at particular applications. Their versatility and strong performance across many language tasks has made LLMs the most popular foundation model architecture today. Rather than training AI models from scratch for each new task, foundation models allow for efficient fine-tuning on much smaller specialized datasets to adapt them for specific uses.

Generative AI

As previously discussed, LLMs fall under the subset of AI called generative AI. Generative AI refers to systems that can autonomously create new content like text, code, images, video or audio that meaningfully extends beyond their training data. LLMs are a leading example of Generative AI because they can generate original, human-like text after training on large text corpora. Other types of generative AI include systems that generate images, videos, music, 3D shapes, and more, based on analyzing datasets of visual content.

Generative AI, fueled by advances in LLMs, has rapidly risen to prominence given its ability to automate content creation in affordable and customized ways. Unlike most AI, which focuses on analysis and classification, generative AI unlocks creative applications that go beyond training data. However, generative systems require responsible design to avoid harm given their ability to produce misleading content at scale if poorly implemented.

Specialized LLMs

Besides general knowledge models, some organizations have developed more specialized LLMs. Bloomberg recently unveiled BloombergGPT[4], a large language model specially trained on financial data to understand nuanced business and finance language.

With 50 billion parameters trained on 360 billion tokens of financial text (comparable to number of words) and 345 billion tokens of general text, BloombergGPT achieves state-of-the-art results on financial NLP tasks like question answering and named entity recognition.

The model's architecture, domain-specific data, and efficient training enable it to match larger models on some benchmarks. While not released publicly because of ethical concerns, BloombergGPT shows the value of curated in-domain data to create specialized AI systems competitive with general models orders of magnitude larger. As firms adopt AI, expect domain-optimized models like BloombergGPT to drive automation and insights. Specialization trades off broad versatility for targeted strengths.

Besides domain-specific pre-training, some organizations have developed LLMs specialized not just in knowledge but in capabilities aligned with human values.

For example, Anthropic's Constitutional AI[5] model incorporates a technique called Constitutional AI to improve capabilities like honesty, harmless, helpfulness, and avoiding harmful stereotypes. During training, the model is recursively prompted to edit its own responses until they demonstrably uphold principles in Anthropic's Bill of Rights for AI —seeking truth, upholding dignity, and promoting empathy. This technique, inspired by human moral development, aims to impart cooperative, harmless instincts exceeding the training distribution.

Models like Constitutional AI exemplify emerging techniques to potentially imbue LLMs with greater alignment to ethical priorities, not just targeted knowledge. However, leaving the development of ethics and constitutional frameworks to AI startups is unlikely to be the most effective approach to developing safe and ethical AI guardrails.

Open or Closed and Why?

Meta released its open source large language model LLaMA[6] in 2023, with 65 billion parameters trained on massive text and code datasets.

Meta's decision to make LLaMA 2 an open source model available for research and commercial use is important because it allows for greater collaboration, due diligence, and innovation in the field of artificial intelligence. By making Llama available to everyone, Meta is encouraging researchers and developers to experiment with the model and find new and creative ways to use it. This could lead to the development of new applications that we can't even imagine today, and it also leads to stronger auditing and risk management by different communities.

OpenAI has not released their popular GPT-3 model as open source, instead providing API access to the model. There are a few likely reasons for this approach. First, keeping GPT-3 closed allows OpenAI to maintain control over how the model is used, reducing risks like harmful misuse. It also allows them to monetize access to the model through their API. Releasing the 175 billion parameter GPT-3 model openly could raise serious security concerns and negatively impact OpenAI's business model. Finally, as an early leader in LLMs, OpenAI may be hesitant to provide open access to their most advanced models and lose their competitive edge.

Similarly, Anthropic has not open sourced Claude or any of its other proprietary LLMs. As a startup aiming to be a leader in safe and beneficial AI, Anthropic wants to control model access carefully to reduce harms. Making Claude open source could allow malicious use that Anthropic wants to avoid. Anthropic also monetizes its AI services, so giving Claude away for free doesn't align with its business interests. As a startup, Anthropic can't afford to give away its core intellectual property that larger companies like Meta can. Given its focus on AI safety, Anthropic is understandably more cautious about open sourcing its advanced models.

There are reasonable arguments on both sides of open versus closed access to large language models. The optimal path forward may involve balancing openness to enable auditing with controls to manage risks. However, companies have an obligation to be transparent about training data, methods, and provide access to researchers to uphold ethics. With care, the power of these models can be harnessed responsibly for the benefit of all.

Why Scale Matters: The Good, the Bad and the Ugly

Each increase in the scale of LLMs has unlocked new beneficial capabilities and furthered state-of-the-art performance on language tasks. While returns diminish, it appears marginal benefits continue well into the hundreds of billions or trillions of parameters. Greater scale enables stronger few-shot learning, knowledge retention over more domains, and more human-like conversation and reasoning. Recent LLMs can rival average human performance on university entrance exams taken cold.

However, scale also confers concerning capabilities like generating harmful, toxic, or biased content at higher fidelity. Mitigating these risks remains an active area of research. Responsible development and deployment of ever-larger models requires care, caution, and close communication with impacted communities.

The lack of transparency regarding training data sources and the methods used can be problematic. For example, algorithmic filtering of training data can skew representations in subtle ways. Attempts to remove overt toxicity by keyword filtering can disproportionately exclude positive portrayals of marginalized groups[7]. Responsible data curation requires first acknowledging and then addressing these complex tradeoffs through input from impacted communities.

Additionally, it is critical to recognize the limitations of LLMs from a consumer perspective. LLMs only possess statistical knowledge about word patterns, not true comprehension of ideas, facts, or emotions. Their fluency can create an illusion of human-like understanding, but rigorous testing reveals brittleness. Just because a LLM can generate coherent text about medicine or law doesn't mean it grasps those professional domains. It does not. Responsible evaluation is essential to avoid overestimating capabilities.

As an example, Meta's Galactica[8] was announced on November 15, 2022. It was a LLM designed to help scientists with their research by summarizing academic papers, solving math problems, generating Wiki articles, writing scientific code, and annotating molecules and proteins. Galactica was trained on a dataset of 48 million scientific papers, textbooks, and websites.

However, Galactica was met with criticism almost immediately after its release. Scientists and tech journalists pointed out[9] that Galactica was producing incorrect and biased output. For example, Galactica claimed that the history of bears in space began in 1963, when a Soviet cosmonaut took a bear into orbit. This isn't true. The first bear in space was actually a French bear named Flic, who was launched into space in 1961.

In addition, Galactica was found to be generating fake data. For example, one user asked Galactica to summarize a paper on the history of quantum mechanics. Galactica responded with a summary that was full of factual errors.

After three days of criticism, Meta pulled Galactica offline. The company said that it was taking Galactica offline to "fix some bugs and improve the quality of the output."

Dr. Emily M. Bender coined the term "non-information spill"[10] to describe the proliferation of synthetic media, such as AI-generated text and images, polluting the online information ecosystem. Bender explains that just as oil spills cause environmental damage, non-information spills like the release of flawed chatbots create systemic harms. The spread of convincing but false content makes it harder to find and trust real information sources. Bender argues that individual efforts at information hygiene must be coupled with regulation, like required watermarking, to clean up this non-information spill.

For businesses, it is vital to embed ethical checkpoints in workflows, allowing models to be stopped if unacceptable risks emerge. The apparent ease of building capable LLMs with existing foundations can mask serious robustness gaps. However unrealistic the scenario may seem under pressure, responsible LLM work requires pragmatic commitments to stop if red lines are crossed during risk assessment.

In summary, while scale enables remarkable progress in language AI, we must maintain realistic perspectives on limitations and employ robust oversight to ensure ethical, responsible development as models grow more capable.

Key Stages of Development

Large language models go through several key stages of development to learn language skills.

The first stage is **pre-training**. In pre-training, the LLM trains on massive datasets of unlabeled text from sources like websites and books. This dataset contains hundreds of billions of words. Pre-training exposes the model to a huge range of language examples to learn the fundamentals of how language works. This stage teaches the LLM general linguistic knowledge and representations of language structure and use.

The second stage is **fine-tuning**. In fine-tuning, the model trains on human-labeled examples for specialized tasks. For instance, it may train on questions and answers to learn question answering. This stage tunes the model to excel at specific applications versus just general language modeling. However, fine-tuning on limited labeled data risks overfitting. Overfitting means the model becomes so tuned to the fine-tuning data that it fails to generalize well. Broad pre-training helps avoid overfitting.

The third stage for some models is **reinforcement learning from human feedback**. Here, the LLM interacts with real users and gets feedback on its responses. It then iteratively improves based on that feedback. This stage helps refine soft skills, like making conversations more engaging, helpful, and safe.

The fourth emerging stage is **efficient adaptation techniques**. These techniques allow updating models for new uses without extensive retraining from scratch. This enables responsively adapting LLMs for new applications as they emerge.

Together, these developmental stages enable creating LLMs that combine general linguistic knowledge with specialized abilities. Pre-training, fine-tuning, reinforcement learning, and efficient adaptation unlock the tremendous potential of large language models in a scalable yet responsible manner.

Training Challenges

Developing large language models poses notable technical and ethical challenges that companies must responsibly address:

- Training is highly computationally intensive, often using thousands of GPUs for extended periods, resulting in substantial energy consumption and carbon emissions. Companies should invest in optimizing efficiency and utilizing renewable energy sources.

- Curating the massive datasets required is expensive in terms of web scraping, human generation, and annotation. Synthetic data and user feedback may help reduce costs, but maintaining data quality is critical.

- Training stability and reproducibility is difficult as small code changes can significantly impact results. Extensive monitoring, debugging protocols, and version control are important to control variability.

- Effectively testing and auditing model logic grows more challenging as scale increases. Greater transparency into model decision processes and representations is needed to verify safety.

- Larger models increase certain risks if improperly developed, including potential training data memorization, inherited biases, and susceptibility to attacks. Rigorous security and testing methodologies are essential.

- Finally, even properly trained models may enable downstream misuse. Reasonable policies to restrict harmful applications warrant careful consideration.

Responsible LLM development requires substantial investments to address technical complexities, promote transparency, mitigate risks, and ensure these powerful systems benefit society. Cross-functional collaboration and ethical engineering practices are key.

Build or Buy?

Many businesses are exploring how to effectively adopt large language models. A key question is whether to build a custom LLM from scratch or start with an existing base model.

A base LLM refers to a pre-trained, publicly available model like GPT-3 or LLaMA 2 that provides general language capabilities. Building on top of these base models can save significant time and resources compared to developing a new LLM from zero. Fine-tuning a base LLM adapts it to a company's specific use case, like customer service chatbots.

The pros of fine-tuning a base LLM are faster implementation, lower compute costs, and leveraging existing capabilities. The cons are less customizability and reliance on external models.

Building a custom LLM enables tight control over training data and objectives. But it demands extensive data curation, engineering, compute resources, significant budget, and time.

Most organizations are apt to start by fine-tuning base LLMs, then potentially train custom models later for core competencies once workflow integration matures. Blending pre-trained models with specialized in-house LLMs tailored to business domains may offer an optimal balance. But assessing needs, resources, and risks is key in determining the right LLM adoption strategy.

Conclusion

The rapid evolution of LLMs invites a closer look at their expanding capabilities while also causing vigilance regarding potential risks.

Businesses exploring applications should maintain realistic perspectives on today's limitations around reasoning, factuality, and bias.

However, LLMs also offer a versatile platform to enhance workflows—if deployed thoughtfully. The path ahead remains open to deliberate, ethical co-shaping between humans and technology.

3

HOW LLMS UNDERSTAND LANGUAGE: DEMYSTIFYING LLM ARCHITECTURES

I n the previous chapter, I summarized the rapid evolution of large language models, highlighting key innovations that have led to today's functionalities and applications. Now I will dive deeper into the technical architectures underlying modern LLMs to breakdown how they achieve such remarkable performance on diverse natural language tasks.

Specifically, I will focus my attention on transformer neural networks, the paradigm-shifting advancement in neural network design that has catalyzed the explosion in LLM scale and capability since 2018. I will explain the core components of the transformer architecture, like self-attention and feedforward networks, that impart these models with exceptional linguistic comprehension.

Additionally, I will explore how design choices in constructing transformer-based LLMs enable different functionalities, discussing tradeoffs between generalizability versus specialization. I will also examine responsible development principles as model scale and complexity increases, emphasizing needs for transparency, robustness, and ethical alignment.

By demystifying the inner workings of modern LLMs' advanced architectures, I aim to support readers as you evaluate capabilities and limitations, facilitate informed adoption, and ensure LLMs benefit diverse stakeholders. Though abstraction enables application without deep architectural knowledge, developing nuanced understanding supports prudent, socially conscious deployment of these transformative technologies.

Transformers

As previously discussed, large language models leverage a category of neural network called transformers to analyze and generate natural language. Transformers have driven explosive progress in capabilities like accurately translating between languages, summarizing long articles, and holding human-like conversations.

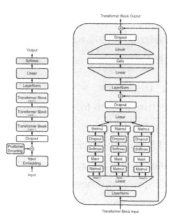

The original GPT model[67]

But how do transformers make sense of language compared to humans? Let's explore a simplified explanation of some key technical innovations that enable their linguistic aptitude.

Tokenization: Representing Words as Numbers

Humans naturally assign meanings to words based on cultural and linguistic backgrounds. We understand subtle differences in meaning and context. Computers, on the other hand, only understand numbers.

This is where tokenization comes in. It's the process of turning text into numeric data. One simple way is assigning a unique ID to each word. For instance, "hello" might be 1, "world" is 2, and so on.

Another technique involves breaking words into smaller parts, called subwords. This can be prefixes, roots, or suffixes. By giving these subwords unique IDs, the system can piece together unfamiliar or complex words. The term "representation" might be divided into "re-pres-ent-ation".

Why use subwords? They help in a couple of ways:

1. Flexibility and Efficiency: By focusing on word parts, the system can tackle words it hasn't seen before or even misspelled words. It can also process information more efficiently. For example, "training" and "trainer" could share the common root "train".

2. Size Matters: Subwords limit the vocabulary size the model needs, making processing more efficient. However, there's a balance to strike. While smaller subwords can address rare or unfamiliar words, they might sometimes lose a bit of the word's context and can require more computational resources.

Real-world applications showcase this concept's adaptability:

- **Novel AI**[11] is shaping AI tools for storytelling. Their custom subword tokenizer enhances storytelling by diving into detailed word fragments. This means capturing more subtle story elements. Plus, their method compresses text better than many competitors, allowing for richer narratives without losing context.

- **BloombergGPT**[4] is tailored for financial contexts. Instead of standard subword methods, it uses unigram tokenization. This method probabilistically picks the best token split based on the surrounding text. The result? A system finely attuned to financial jargon and nuances.

In essence, tokenization translates human language into a format that computer systems can work with, making it a cornerstone for advanced linguistic models.

Embeddings: Words as Points in Space

Once words are tokenized as numbers, the next step is mapping those arbitrary numbers into meaningful math representations. This happens in embedding layers.

Embeddings map each token ID number to a point in a high-dimensional vector space. These spaces have hundreds or even thousands of dimensions, beyond our usual understanding of 3D space, encapsulating the vast richness of language.

Remarkably, words with related meanings end up clustered together in regions of this vector space. For example, "king" and "queen" may be points next to each other, while totally unrelated words are distant.

These spatial relationships emerge organically through training, as the model learns latent patterns between words based on their usage in billions of sentences. The relative positioning encodes the nuanced semantic connection between terms.

This allows transformers to represent mathematically similarities and differences between words based on distance measurements between their embedding points. Words closer in the embedding space are more semantically related based on past context.

This is similar to how humans build mental maps of related concepts through accumulated experience. Embedding spaces provide an efficient mathematical representation that captures core aspects of meaning.

However, not all embedding techniques are one-size-fits-all. Depending on the specific task or use case, different embedding techniques and optimizations can be used to yield better results. Let's revisit semantic search, covered in the previous chapter.

Search systems aim to retrieve the most relevant documents or content based on a user's query. The traditional method involves indexing each document based on keywords. However, keyword-based search can miss out on contextually relevant results that may not contain the exact terms but are semantically related. Here, embeddings can play a crucial role.

Imagine you run a travel website where users can search for information on destinations, travel tips, hotel reviews, and more. You want to ensure that when users type in their search queries, they get the most relevant articles and information, even if they don't use the exact keywords present in the content.

Anna, a user on your site, types in the query: "quiet beach spots in Bali."

Without using embeddings:

Your system might simply look for articles with the exact words "quiet," "beach," "spots," and "Bali." This might cause Anna to miss out on an excellent article titled "Serene Seashores: Bali's Hidden Gems." because it doesn't have the words "quiet" or "spots."

With embeddings:

Your system understands the context and meaning behind Anna's search. The word "serene" in the article is recognized as semantically close to "quiet," and "seashores" is related to "beach spots."

Anna's search will now retrieve the "Serene Seashores: Bali's Hidden Gems" article, providing her with relevant content that she would have missed with a basic keyword search.

This simple enhancement using embeddings offers Anna a better user experience, ensuring she finds what she's truly looking for, even if she doesn't use the exact words present in the content.

Here are some real-world applications:

- **Semantic Search Engines:** Modern search engines like Google have shifted from purely keyword-based methods to semantic search, understanding the context behind queries. They leverage advanced embedding techniques to match user intent with relevant content.

- **E-commerce Recommendations:** Platforms like Amazon use embeddings to understand user search queries and recommend products that might not have the exact term in their title or description but are contextually related and relevant.

- **Legal and Medical Search:** In fields with technical language, the context is crucial. Embedding-based search systems can provide more accurate results

by understanding the semantic relationships
between complex terms.

In conclusion, embeddings have revolutionized how systems understand and process language. However, by tailoring and optimizing these embeddings for specific applications like search, we can ensure even more accurate and meaningful interactions. By understanding these nuances, businesses can better leverage the power of modern language models to meet specific needs, providing users with more relevant and intuitive experiences.

Attention Mechanisms: Learning to Focus

Now that words are represented as points in space as embeddings, the next challenge is analyzing their complex relationships within sentences to infer meaning.

Attention mechanisms[2] are a breakthrough enabling just this—identifying which words provide important context. The model learns patterns about which words to focus on more strongly versus those that can be glossed over.

Think of attention mechanisms as the lens of a camera, zooming in on the most important parts of a scene. It prioritizes key subjects while softly blurring out the background, even though the background remains part of the overall picture.

For example, as humans read a sentence, we pay closer attention to substantively relevant words compared to generic articles and prepositions that play a grammatical role. Attention allows models to learn these focuses.

Words assigned higher relevance receive greater weight, enabling extracting meaning by concentrating on salient parts of text. Lower weighted words still retain reduced influence.

This selective attention provides huge improvements in comprehending language sequences compared to approaches treating all words equally. The model directs limited capacity towards the most useful parts.

Self-attention: Building Global Understanding

Self-attention extends attention mechanisms to relate all words within a text sequence rather than just considering immediately adjacent words.

This equips models with a more human-like global comprehension of semantic contexts. For example, self-attention can directly relate the word "student" to "teacher" in a sentence about students asking questions in class. This captures meaning that depends on non-local dependencies.

Let's break this down with another example:

- In the sentence, "The boy, who was sitting on the bench with a book, waved to his friend," the main action is "The boy waved to his friend."

- The clause "who was sitting on the bench with a book" provides extra information about the boy, but the words "boy" and "waved" are separated by this clause.

- The relationship between "boy" and "waved" is a non-local dependency because they are not immediately next to each other but are semantically related.

Additionally, multi-headed self-attention employs multiple attention layers in parallel. This allows jointly focusing on different types of relationships from multiple perspectives - such as meaning, syntax, entities, etc.

Imagine having multiple camera lenses observing the same scene but from different angles, capturing multiple perspectives. This is what multi-headed self-attention does — focusing on diverse aspects of the same text.

Together, these inter-related attention heads provide transformers with a multidimensional representation of the relationships between all words, anywhere in a text sequence. This enables robust global reasoning.

Limiting Focus with Context Length

However, processing arbitrarily long sequences with full attention becomes computationally infeasible. So transformers restrict active attention to a window of recent context.

For example, some smaller models may only actively focus on the last 512 words at once, while the largest models like Claude 2 can now handle over 150,000 words of context in its attention window at a time. This allows Claude 2 to build understanding over hundreds of pages of text. Longer context windows generally improve capability but require more compute.

As this window slides forward word-by-word, previous words outside the window become memories that can still be retrieved if relevant. Attention is focused on the most recent contexts while retaining ability to reference broader memory.

This provides an efficient balance: localized attention combined with global memory. Transformers exhibit human-like reading comprehension through similar mechanisms—focused attention augmented by summarizing broader themes.

Building Deep Linguistic Models

In addition to special mechanisms for focusing on specific parts of text (like when we pay close attention to certain words or phrases), transformers also have what we can think of as assembly lines that process word representations. It's similar to how factories process raw materials to build something meaningful, just as we assemble LEGO bricks to create structures.

Think of it like building LEGO models. The word representations are like the simple LEGO bricks. On their own, they represent individual words. But when processed in these factory-like layers, they begin to form more intricate patterns and structures, aiding the model in understanding language at a deeper level.

These assembly lines, or neural network layers, start piecing these bricks together into simple structures like walls or towers, representing the basic rules of how words mesh together. As we introduce more layers, these models grow more elaborate, constructing windows, doors, roofs, and eventually entire houses. This process mirrors how the layers learn progressively more advanced concepts, going from understanding mere phrases to entire documents.

By stacking these layers atop one another, transformers gain the ability to grasp increasingly intricate linguistic ideas. The many layers allow the models to derive meanings from a wider context, not just individual words.

While the earlier layers might zero in on simpler sentence structures, the later ones piece together broader themes by connecting key words from different parts of the text. Thus, more layers equate to a richer understanding of the training data.

To illustrate, while the foundational layers might detect basic grammar patterns in a sentence, the more advanced layers could discern the overarching theme of an extended passage by drawing connections between scattered keywords.

However, when using traditional methods to train these deep stacks of layers, challenges arise. Imagine a conveyor belt moving LEGO bricks. As it stretches, it might slow down so much that hardly any bricks advance, or small hitches might lead to widespread failures, spilling bricks everywhere. Both scenarios hinder the effective training of a valuable model.

To address this, transformers incorporate 'residual connections'. Picture these as ramps or shortcuts that bypass certain steps in the assembly line, ensuring the smooth progression of our LEGO bricks. Such shortcuts prevent the process from stalling or breaking down unexpectedly.

While many transformers are designed with a few dozen layers, these residual connections even allow for training models that boast over 100 layers. This capability equips them with an immense depth, enabling them to depict complex linguistic ideas by recognizing relationships between distant words in a text.

Several state-of-the-art language models have been developed in recent years, each with varying architecture depths. Not all developers disclose details, but I can share a few examples. For instance, OpenAI's GPT-3[12] has 96 layers in its largest variant, while BERT[13], developed by Google, has models with 12 layers in its base version, and 24 layers in its large version. The depth of these models—represented by the number of layers—often correlates with their capacity to understand and generate intricate linguistic constructs, though the sheer number of layers isn't the sole determinant of a model's performance.

Expanding Capacity and Knowledge

The number of trainable parameters within a transformer largely determines its knowledge capacity—how much information it might absorb and recall during learning.

Parameters are essentially adjustable dials that determine how the model will process different words and sentences during training. Initial random values are incrementally tuned by exposing the model to billions of words from books, websites, and other texts over successive updates.

The final parameter settings encode all the statistical relationships, contexts, and knowledge that the model distills from the training process. More parameters provide greater capacity for nuance and complexity.

But as we tread into the realm of larger and larger models, we're also stepping into uncharted ethical waters. Their vast knowledge and understanding make even more critical to ensure these models are trained responsibly and don't inadvertently perpetuate biases or misinformation.

Variations in Architectures: Navigating the Strategic Choices

Business leaders may encounter terms like "encoder-only," "decoder-only," and "encoder-decoder" models. These describe key architectural differences:

- **Encoder-Only:** Encoders digest volumes of text into deep understandings, like an analyst deriving insights from market data. For example, Google's BERT has 110 million parameters and was trained on Wikipedia and books. Encoders excel at comprehension-focused tasks like search, sentiment analysis, and classification.

- **Decoder-Only:** Decoders produce an eloquent text from prompts, like a wordsmith crafting press releases. For instance, GPT-3 has over 175 billion parameters and was trained on internet text. Decoders are ideal for generative applications like conversational AI, content creation, and communication.

- **Encoder-Decoder:** Combining encoders and decoders enables reading comprehension plus relevant text generation, like a strategist analyzing issues and devising solutions. Encoder-decoder models translate between languages, summarize reports into briefs, answer nuanced questions, and more.

While fundamentally a decoder, GPT-3 develops a strong contextual understanding comparable to encoders. Its vast scale and training enables encoders' strengths without separate encoding components. GPT-3 generates coherently by holistically contemplating prompts. This exemplifies modern LLMs' flexibility—with sufficient data and compute, capabilities transcend rigid architectural boundaries.

There is no universally superior architecture. Each provides advantages based on tradeoffs:

- Encoders require less data/compute but cannot smoothly generate text.

- Decoders produce remarkably human-like writing but need massive training.

- Encoder-decoders balance fluent generation with comprehension.

Unidirectional vs. Bidirectional Models

Just like in our human conversations, the sequence, or the order of words, can significantly impact meaning. This leads us to an important distinction in how some models process these sequences:

Unidirectional Models:

Think about reading a book, and you're only allowed to remember what you've read so far, without sneaking a peek at the upcoming pages. Unidirectional models operate in a similar manner. They process and predict based on the preceding context. So, if our model was predicting the next word in the sentence "The cat climbed up the ___," it would use the information from "The cat climbed up the" but wouldn't consider any words that might come after.

Bidirectional Models:

Now, imagine you could read both previous and upcoming pages of a book to understand the current page better. That's how bidirectional models work. They incorporate both past and future context when understanding or predicting tokens. Using the same example, a bidirectional model would consider words both before and after "the ___" to make its prediction, giving it a broader context.

This ability of bidirectional models to look both ways provides a richer understanding of text, capturing relationships that might be missed in a purely unidirectional approach. However, there's a trade-off. While bidirectional models are great for tasks like comprehension and classification, their 'peeking into the future' nature makes them less straightforward for generative tasks, like continuing a given text, because they rely on information that isn't available in a true generative scenario.

By understanding these distinctions, we can appreciate the architectural choices made in different language models, tailoring their design to specific tasks, be it understanding text or generating new content.

Vocabulary Selection

At this point, you might be wondering, how do models decide which words to focus on or include? The heart of this question lies in the intricacies of vocabulary selection.

Picture a library with limited shelf space, but an unlimited supply of books. The librarian has to choose which books to place on the shelves for readers. Similarly, when building a language model, there's a limit to the number of words (or tokens) that can be effectively managed. This selection of words is the model's vocabulary.

But how do we choose these words?

- **Common Words:** Just like bestsellers that occupy prime space in a library, typical words from the vast expanse of the internet get priority. These are the words we use in everyday conversations or writing.

- **Technical & Topical Terms:** However, just like specialized books in our library analogy, some words are more niche, specific to certain topics or technical fields. In an expansive model, there might be limited representation for these. Imagine an architecture book in a library predominantly filled with mystery novels. The specific jargon and concepts in the architecture book might not get as much attention.

The process of vocabulary selection is thus both an art and a science. It shapes what concepts and nuances the model can represent, understand, and generate. The choice of words included (or excluded) in the vocabulary can greatly influence a model's expertise in certain domains, its generalizability, and its blind spots.

So, while the underlying architecture and learning mechanisms are crucial, the very words these models learn from play a foundational role. It's akin to ensuring our library doesn't just have bestsellers, but also essential reads from varied domains, providing a balanced and comprehensive knowledge base.

Let's deep dive into LLM vocabulary in practice:

1. Generalist LLM - GPT (by OpenAI)

Akin to a public library that stocks a diverse range of books, GPT has been trained on vast sections of the internet. Its vocabulary is broad and covers a wide spectrum of topics.

It's useful for a variety of general tasks, such as conversational AI, content generation, and summarization across many domains.

However, while it can touch upon many topics, its depth on highly specialized subjects might be limited compared to domain-specific models.

2. Legal LLM - LegalBERT (adapted from BERT for legal texts)

Like a law library, LegalBERT is saturated with legal jargon, case references, and terminologies pertinent to the legal field.

It excels in understanding legal documents, contracts, and court case summaries, assisting lawyers in legal research and analysis.

The specialized vocabulary provides insights into complex legal nuances, a feat challenging for generic LLMs.

These examples show that while a generalist LLM like GPT-3 is a jack-of-all-trades, there are domain-specific LLMs finely tuned for particular sectors. Their vocabularies have been crafted to offer depth, precision, and the illusion of expertise in their respective domains, making them useful assets for specialized tasks. However, these domain-specific LLMs are still just statistical representations of words, not reasoning engines that fully understand the topics they cover.

Base Model vs Fine-tuned Model Architectures

Base models provide broad foundations, like a consultant with multi-industry knowledge. For example, GPT-3 excels at general tasks like content creation, without additional training beyond its original pre-training.

Fine-tuning then specializes models by training on niche datasets, transforming generalists into industry language experts. For instance, GPT-3, fined-tuned on legal documents, generates specialized drafts using legal jargon and concepts. Medical LLMs finessed on research texts answer intricate patient queries.

The Path to True Language Intelligence

Modern transformer-based design provides a versatile, efficient architecture to imbue models with strong linguistic pattern recognition based on statistical learning over massive datasets.

Their capacity for contextual attention, deep representation, and knowledge retention drives exponential progress in language generation and comprehension. However, transformers remain domain-limited, brittle, and biased without true semantic understanding.

Integrating grounded human oversight, robust ethics review, and complementary technologies addressing limitations provides a principled path forward.

4

THE ART OF INFERENCE PARAMETERS

In the realm of AI, especially when working with large language models, "inference" is the phase when we ask the model to generate or predict content based on its training. Have you ever wondered how we can influence the LLM to craft content the way we desire during inference time? The secret lies in a set of configurations called 'inference parameters'. In this chapter, I'll peel back the curtain on some of these configurations and show how they help us shape the LLM's output for our specific needs.

The Length Limit: Max New Tokens

Think of 'max new tokens' as instructing an author about the length of a chapter. It's simply a way to tell the model how long or short we want its response to be.

Example: If you're looking for a quick tweet, you'd set a small value, like 50 tokens. For a longer blog post intro, you might choose 200 tokens. Just remember, like telling an author a word limit, the model might sometimes conclude sooner.

In a model like the LLM, each token represents a chunk of information, which might be as short as a character or as long as a word. By setting a limit on the number of tokens, we're essentially setting a computational budget. Limiting tokens ensures that the model doesn't exceed computational or context window constraints, while still attempting to provide meaningful content within that boundary.

The Path of Least Resistance: Greedy Decoding

Greedy decoding is like a writer always choosing the most obvious word next in a sentence. They pick the most predictable, safe option every time.

Example: In predicting the end of the sentence "The sun is...", the model might choose "...shining" because it's a common and safe completion.

Greedy decoding is a deterministic approach. At each step, the model calculates the probabilities of all possible next tokens (based on its training data) and simply chooses the one with the highest probability. While this is computationally efficient, it doesn't always produce the most diverse or nuanced outputs since it's always aiming for the most likely next step.

A Pinch of Randomness: Random Sampling

In random sampling, each word (or token) is picked based on its probability, but not necessarily the most probable one. This can be visualized as spinning a weighted roulette wheel, where the segments for each word are sized according to their probabilities.

Example:

For the phrase "The sun is...", let's consider the model's predicted next tokens and their probabilities:

- shining: 50%
- setting: 25%
- playing: 0.5%
- hot: 1%
- bright: 0.8%
- ... (and more options with smaller probabilities)

If you visualize these probabilities on a roulette wheel:

- The segment for "shining" would cover half the wheel because of its 50% probability.
- "Setting" might cover a quarter of it.
- "Playing" would have a much smaller segment, etc.

When the wheel is spun, it is most likely to land on "shining", but there's a chance it could land on "playing" or any of the other options.

For the phrase "The sun is...", using greedy decoding, the LLM would always choose "shining" because it has the highest probability. But with random sampling, there's a possibility that the LLM might sometimes pick "playing" (despite its lower probability) and end up generating the continuation "...playing hide and seek behind the clouds." This can produce more diverse and creative outputs.

However, it's worth noting that while this method ensures diversity in outputs, there's a trade-off: the outputs can occasionally be less coherent or contextually appropriate since the highest probability choice isn't always picked.

Filtering the Choices: Top-k and Top-p Sampling

These methods are like giving our AI artist a palette with selected colors (words) to paint with.

Top-k Sampling

The model considers only the 'k' most probable next tokens, ignoring the rest. This introduces a balance between total randomness and greedy selection.

Example:

Let's say for the phrase "The apple is...", the model's next token predictions and their probabilities are:

- red: 4%
- green: 3%
- ripe: 2%
- juicy: 0.5%
- tart: 0.3%
- shiny: 0.1%
- ... (and many more with smaller probabilities)

If we set k=3, the model will consider only the top 3 probable words. In this case, "red", "green", and "ripe" would be chosen, and the probabilities would be normalized among these.

Top-p Sampling

Instead of a fixed number of top tokens, the model considers a dynamic set of tokens whose combined probability exceeds a threshold 'p'. This ensures a level of unpredictability while also eliminating extremely unlikely, and potentially nonsensical, choices.

Using the above probabilities:

If we set p = 6%, then:

red (4%) + green (3%) = 7% (which exceeds 6%)

In this case, "red" and "green" would be chosen. If we increased p to 7%, "ripe" would also be included, since:

red (4%) + green (3%) + ripe (2%) = 9% (which exceeds 7%)

The primary difference is that top-k has a fixed number of choices, while top-p allows for a variable number of choices depending on their probabilities.

Adjusting the Creative Thermostat: Temperature

Temperature dictates the level of creativity or randomness in the model's response. Imagine a chef adjusting the heat while cooking; higher heat (higher temperature) means bolder flavors (more creativity,) while lower heat leads to milder outcomes.

Simplified Example: With a low temperature setting, our phrase "The sky at sunset is..." might usually end with "...beautiful". Crank up that temperature, and you might get "...a canvas of dreams."

For a temperature of $T=1$

- beautiful: 3%
- orange: 2%
- darkening: 1%
- a canvas of dreams: 0.5%
- ... (and more options)

For a temperature of T=0.5 (low temperature)

- beautiful: 6%
- orange: 4%
- darkening: 2%
- a canvas of dreams: 1%
- ... (amplified values)

Consequently, "beautiful" would have an even higher probability, and the model would most likely pick it.

However, for a high temperature, say T=2, "a canvas of dreams" becomes more probable, leading to a more creative output.

- beautiful: 1.5%
- orange: 1%
- darkening: 0.5%
- a canvas of dreams: 0.25%
- ... (scaled down values)

This scaled-down version makes the difference between the probabilities less pronounced.

Think of temperature as a "dial" that controls the model's level of confidence. At its basic setting (a value of 1), the model responds in the way it's most trained to. Turn the dial up (above 1), and the model becomes more experimental, sometimes offering surprising answers. Turn it down (below 1), and the model sticks closer to what it thinks is the most expected answer, being more cautious. It's like adjusting the seasoning in a dish; a little change can make a big difference in the flavor.

Conclusion

Understanding these inference parameters equips us to better harness the creative prowess of the LLM. It's less about the technical jargon and more about knowing the levers and dials we can adjust to make it work for us.

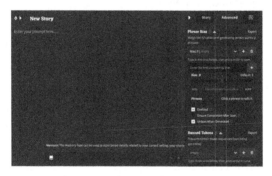

Novel AI's user configurable inference parameters

Some apps, like Novel AI—a writing co-pilot—allow users to adjust the dials to best achieve their goals. This complements the prompt, giving end users more ways to get the best out of the base LLM.

5

APPROPRIATE USE CASES FOR LLMS: A NUANCED PERSPECTIVE

Large language models demonstrate remarkable fluency and versatility when thoughtfully prompted. However, their statistical nature means outputs lack robust reasoning. This chapter explores responsible use cases that play to LLMs' strengths as aids, not autonomous experts. I spotlight promising applications in areas like education, search, and coding where LLMs excel at augmenting human capabilities. However, each section also examines limitations requiring judicious implementation. My guidance emphasizes framing LLMs as useful but fallible tools requiring ongoing human guidance.

Creative Inspiration

LLMs truly excel at fluid generation of creative prose, code, and ideas when provided with prompts containing seed content. Their ability to continue patterns statistically combined with stochastic sampling produces immense original material.

The term "stochastic sampling"[21] refers to the random element in how LLMs generate multiple possible continuations of a prompt. It's akin to tossing a pair of dice—you can't predict the exact numbers that will come up, but the range of possibilities is finite. Similarly, when prompted, a LLM randomly selects words to form original responses within the scope of patterns learned during training. By producing varied options in this probabilistic way, rather than a single deterministic output, LLMs can increase the novelty and diversity of generated content.

Users creatively riffing with LLMs report greatly enhanced productivity and inspiration for writing. Open-ended riffing with models amplifies human imagination and stimulates new connections between concepts.

However, this creative potential raises important copyright and ethical considerations. Often, LLMs are trained on vast datasets that include copyrighted materials, like books and articles. This training process might infringe on the rights of artists, authors, and other content creators, leading to significant legal and ethical quandaries.

Fan fiction writers noticed[14] AI startup Sudowrite displaying suspiciously detailed knowledge of niche tropes and terminology. Terms that are nonsensical outside of their fan spaces. The model's familiarity with these hyper-specific elements proves it was trained on fanfic content without proper attribution or consent, leading to outcry in online creator communities. While the fan fiction stories are derivative works, these hobbyist writers don't profit from their legal creative outlet. This highlights the need for a far more careful ethical review of training data sources and attribution practices with generative AI models.

It's imperative that companies prioritize the ethical sourcing of their training data, ensuring it respects copyrights and intellectual property rights. With thoughtful data practices, LLMs can unlock human creativity without exploiting the work of others.

Conversational Aid

Today's LLMs excel at continuing conversational patterns in a natural, engaging way when prompted effectively. Their versatility allows them to cover a wide range of topics and respond appropriately to small talk, simple questions, and other common user interactions. While coherence and accuracy still falter in long, complex conversations, LLMs are well-suited for helpful conversational agents that aim to provide users with useful information efficiently.

For example, a LLM-powered chatbot on a company's website could answer basic customer service FAQs by pattern matching user questions to common responses. This allows rapidly addressing many routine user needs. However, errors and contradictions can emerge when conversations go off-script.

Additional techniques should complement the conversational strengths of LLMs:

- Retrieval augmentation[15] combines LLMs with real-world data from APIs, databases, and knowledge bases to ground responses in facts instead of just text patterns. For example, a customer service chatbot could query an internal database to retrieve a user's purchase history and order status before responding to their question.

This allows the chatbot to augment its natural language capabilities with accurate, personalized data like order details and shipping dates. This results in responses grounded in specific facts about the user rather than just replies generated from the text patterns the LLM was trained on. In this way, retrieval augmentation complements the conversational strengths of LLMs with factual precision.

- Ensemble models[16] blend outputs from multiple LLMs to improve overall accuracy.

- Ongoing training on logs of real customer interactions further tunes performance.

With the right complementary technologies and human oversight, LLMs can enable more natural, productive conversational experiences between users and AI systems focused on efficient information exchange. Their strengths make them valuable aids, but human guidance and supplementary techniques are essential for overcoming inherent limitations.

Background Knowledge

Large language models contain expansive world knowledge that allows them to summarize concisely the key themes and concepts around a complex topic. This enables efficiently providing users with an informative background context to orient them before diving into specifics. For example, a LLM can overview the major events, figures, and high-level timeline of World War 2 to onboard a reader new to the topic.

While great for summarizing topical breadth, LLMs often miss or misstate key facts due to imprecision. Combining retrieval augmentation from structured data sources with LLM generation allows cementing the overview with concrete details. The LLM overview orients the reader, while retrieved statistics, timelines, examples, and definitions ground the summary in precision. Further techniques like human review of final summaries can additionally enhance accuracy.

With the right complementary techniques, LLM-generated background summaries can engage users with high-level topical knowledge while also integrating precise factual details through retrieval. This hybrid approach provides orientation along with grounding.

Augmenting Search & QA

Large language models have shown great skill in interpreting the intent behind complex, wordy questions. This natural language capability makes LLMs useful aids for search engines and question answering systems, which can struggle to parse long, ambiguous human queries. A LLM can rephrase meandering questions into simple, clear queries that better convey what information the user wants. For example, a verbose question about mortgage rates could be distilled to "What are current 30-year fixed mortgage rates?" This allows search systems to more accurately retrieve relevant results and answers.

To understand how LLMs can further enhance search, it's important to revisit embeddings covered in the previous chapter. Embeddings are vector representations of words where words with similar meanings are mapped to points close together in vector space. This enables models to understand semantic similarities between words.

For example, keywords like "car", "automobile", and "vehicle" would have embedding representations near each other, even though they are different words.

Compare this to traditional keyword search:

- Keyword search indexes documents and queries based on matching exact terms. So a search for "car" would only match pages with that exact word, missing synonyms.

- Embedding search understands semantic similarity between words like "car" and "automobile" based on their embeddings being close together. So a query for "car" would also match pages with the word "automobile", increasing recall. The same applies to phrases, where "What's your name?" and "My name is Flora." will be closer together than "Who won the World Cup?"

By understanding semantics, embeddings allow search engines to match user intent with relevant content even when keywords don't exactly overlap.

Some businesses are enhancing LLMs with programming to handle reasoning for certain logic-based questions. These "program-aided LLMs"[17] have shown promise on limited types of questions requiring steps like mathematical operations. However, they still require extensive human guidance to function properly across a wide range of question answering.

Additional techniques could further aid search and QA systems. Combining facts retrieved from knowledge bases with LLM-generated query interpretations may improve comprehension. Training LLMs on logs of real user questions can tune them to better match natural search patterns. But human review remains essential to filter out any inaccurate interpretations made by the LLM.

With the right balance of capabilities, LLMs can clarify the intent of complex questions as an aid to search engines and QA systems retrieving final answers. They are most effective as part of a thoughtful ensemble approach.

Low-Stakes Ideation

Divergent ideation for early-stage brainstorming benefits greatly from LLMs' ability to offer wide-ranging relevant completions. Their stochasticity and lack of critical judgment encourage free association exploration. However, relying solely on LLM-generated ideas without deeper consideration of ethics, safety, and rationality risks dangerous oversights. LLMs should support but not replace careful deliberative thinking.

Code Suggestions

Research indicates generative AI like Codex can speed up developer productivity through automated code assistance.

By suggesting common syntax, APIs, and patterns, these tools can expedite repetitive coding tasks, enabling developers to focus on higher-value challenges. A study by McKinsey[18] has found 2-3x speed improvements on activities like code documentation and refactoring.

However, experts caution these tools have limitations. For novel, complex tasks requiring custom engineering, gains can diminish considerably. Human oversight remains essential for resolving tricky requirements, ensuring architectural quality, and code review. Generative AI is best used to augment developers rather than replace them.

The ideal role is as an aid that complements skilled programmers. With responsible development principles and human guidance focused on augmentation, code assistance tools can unlock productivity improvements on routine coding without sacrificing rigor. But sole reliance on generative AI risks undesirable results. With the right collaborative integration, these technologies can expand developer capacity while maintaining quality.

However, legal concerns have emerged around AI code generation tools like GitHub Copilot, which uses OpenAI's Codex model. OpenAI trained Codex on billions of lines of public code, including from GitHub repositories. A recent class action lawsuit[19] alleges Copilot violates open source licenses by reproducing licensed code without proper attribution based on its foundations in Codex.

The suit argues this constitutes "software piracy". While defendants Microsoft, GitHub, and OpenAI claim fair use protections, experts note the unsettled legal territory regarding AI training data. Prudence dictates a cautious approach pending these open questions. As with any technology, responsible implementation aligns innovation with stakeholders' rights.

Summarization

LLMs have shown promising ability to summarize lengthy documents into concise overviews capturing key information. Their statistical learning allows identifying central topics and themes by analyzing word patterns across corpora. When provided a long text, the LLM can generate a short summary highlighting the core ideas and events.

This summarization capability makes LLMs useful aids for quickly digesting complex material. For example, an executive could input an extensive business report into a LLM and receive back a succinct high-level summary capturing the key takeaways. This allows efficiently grasping the essence before diving into details.

However, LLM summaries risk inaccuracies and omissions without human oversight. Key facts and figures may be missed or misstated due to the stochastic nature of text generation. Nuanced analysis and conclusions require human judgment, not just statistical word patterns.

LLMs should augment summarization workflows rather than act autonomously. Effective techniques include combining retrieval of key data points with LLM generation. Human review of final summaries to correct errors and fill gaps is essential for accuracy. When used collaboratively, LLMs can accelerate document understanding while maintaining precision.

Writing

LLMs show immense creativity in generating original prose when provided with prompts containing seed content to continue. Their fluency makes them versatile writing aids for both fiction and nonfiction. Many authors report LLMs help overcome writer's block by providing useful suggestions to riff on.

However, ethical and legal concerns around using pirated copyrighted books to train LLMs raise questions for fiction writing, as highlighted in an investigative report by The Atlantic[20]. Generative writing risks implicitly replicating elements from authors whose work was used without consent. More careful sourcing of training data is needed to respect creator rights.

For nonfiction like business writing, LLMs can efficiently produce drafts capturing patterns and themes from source material. But inaccuracies often emerge, needing correction. Key ideas may be missed or misconstrued by the statistical nature of generation. Nuanced analysis requires human insight.

Responsible use cases involve LLMs as aids for suggesting prose humans refine with oversight. Full automation risks low quality and ethical issues. With collaboration, LLMs can enhance writing productivity without sacrificing accuracy or creator rights. But sole reliance on models leaves gaps needing human judgment.

Education Context

Generative AI is shaping the educational landscape in profound ways. Its foray into education has opened the door to dynamic methods of engagement, both for students and educators.

One of the most promising applications is in Intelligent Tutoring Systems. Here, LLMs, with their ability to understand and respond to diverse student queries, offer guidance through intricate topics. This isn't unlike having a personal tutor available around the clock. Moreover, the tedium of designing quizzes manually is now being replaced by LLMs that can spontaneously generate a range of questions for any topic, ensuring students are tested comprehensively. And then there's the prospect of interactive textbooks: envision educational books that engage students in real time, answering their queries, and suggesting relevant content as they learn.

The advantages of infusing education with LLMs are manifold. Their knack for personalizing content could mean each student receives a learning experience tailored to their pace and understanding. What's more, the inherent scalability of LLMs ensures a broad spectrum of students can benefit simultaneously, democratizing quality education. For educators, routine tasks, such as answering common queries, could be offloaded to these models, allowing them to invest time in nuanced teaching aspects. Perhaps the most revolutionary aspect is their potential to democratize education. By making high-quality resources accessible and affordable, underserved communities across the globe can experience enriched learning.

However, it's essential to approach this innovation with a discerning eye. LLMs, being trained on vast and varied datasets, might inadvertently perpetuate biases. They may falter, presenting information that's not entirely accurate, and curating age-appropriate content remains a pressing concern. Also, relying on underserved communities to test unreliable educational methods and low-quality resources is unethical. Understanding this distinction will be crucial as automation grows in educational settings.

Despite the allure of automation, the soul of education remains with human educators. They impart not just knowledge but also emotional support, mentorship, and a human touch that no AI can emulate. While LLMs are great tools, they must be integrated wisely. This includes using vetted datasets to train them, combining stored knowledge with their generative capabilities for a comprehensive response, and consistently monitoring and refining their outputs based on pedagogical feedback.

Appropriate Framing

A major factor in beneficial versus harmful LLM deployment is appropriately framing their role. Depicting LLMs as autonomous results in people overly trusting outputs. Framing LLMs as fallible tools that generate text statistically rather than via structured knowledge encourages healthily skeptical oversight. Just like other statistical text generators like search and recommendation, LLMs produce useful but not definitive outputs for humans to build on thoughtfully.

Wise vigilance comes from preserving humans in the loop rather than fully automated black boxes. LLMs achieve the greatest real-world benefits working in concert with domain experts, analysts, ethicists, and impacted communities. This keeps meaningful human agency in decision processes rather than over-reliance on statistically generated text.

6

UNLOCKING PRODUCTIVITY GAINS FROM GENERATIVE AI

The advent of large language models and other forms of generative AI has sparked extensive discussion on how these technologies could transform business operations.

However, concrete evidence on how these tools affect real-world job performance remains limited. While promising, generative AI is still an emerging technology. Thoughtful research is required to move beyond speculation on its benefits and risks.

Only rigorous studies examining generative AI's impact on employees doing actual work can provide meaningful insights for business leaders planning adoption strategies.

This chapter synthesizes key findings from the latest research investigating generative AI's influence on worker productivity and related outcomes. I summarize results from experiments across domains including customer service, professional writing, programming, and more. The empirical data presents a nuanced perspective, with productivity impacts varying across user skill levels and task types. While positive effects dominate, limitations and implementation challenges also emerge.

Responsible integration strategies balancing productivity objectives with ethics and security considerations are imperative. When deployed judiciously, generative AI can enhance staff capabilities and workplace satisfaction. But imprudent adoption risks unintended consequences.

By examining the evidence to date, business leaders can craft measured plans to capture generative AI's advantages while safeguarding against potential pitfalls.

Quantifying Generative AI's Productivity Impact

Among the first large-scale studies quantifying generative AI's real-world impact, Erik Brynjolfsson, Danielle Li, and Lindsey Raymond analyzed[22] its effects on 5,000 customer service agents at a Fortune 500 software company. The company deployed AI-powered chatbots suggesting responses to customer inquiries based on training data from prior interactions. Employees could choose to use or ignore the AI's recommendations.

With access to the AI, agents resolved 13.8% more customer issues per hour on average, allowing them to juggle more inquiries simultaneously and resolve problems faster. The AI enhanced multitasking and knowledge sharing, permitting less experienced reps to perform at the level of their more tenured peers. Novice agents saw a dramatic 35% productivity boost, while the AI brought negligible gains for top talent whose expertise already embodied the knowledge it provided.

Beyond efficiency, the AI also improved customer satisfaction by guiding more empathetic responses. Overall, the technology appeared to supplement worker strengths rather than replace skills. This provides initial evidence that generative AI may deliver measurable productivity gains in customer service scenarios, especially for developing employees.

Further evidence comes from an experimental study[23] by Shakked Noy and Whitney Zhang at Massachusetts Institute of Technology (MIT). They assessed generative AI's impact on 444 professionals across occupations that involve writing. Participants completed two incentivized 30-minute writing tasks mimicking workplace projects, one unaided and one where a randomly selected half could use ChatGPT. Graduate students blindly assessed the written outputs.

With ChatGPT, participants' writing productivity jumped 59% on average. The AI dramatically reduced the time spent drafting the initial text, allowing greater focus on editing and refinement. The quality of work also increased significantly, according to evaluator ratings. Less skilled writers improved more than those with higher baseline performance, as the AI distributed knowledge.

Though limited in scale, this experiment demonstrates generative AI's promise for enhancing productivity and quality in knowledge work requiring custom writing. The technology amplified human strengths while automating rote aspects of content production.

In the software engineering domain, a study[24] assessed Microsoft's GitHub Copilot, a programming productivity tool that suggests code based on an underlying generative

AI system. Across 17 developers, Copilot increased task completion speed by 62% on average compared to unaided work. Participants also subjectively rated Copilot as increasing their productivity. As in other domains, less experienced engineers benefited more from the AI collaboration.

Overall, these results provide initial evidence generative AI could yield substantial productivity improvements in software development—an increasingly crucial capability as technology permeates business operations.

Synthesizing these studies, access to generative AI boosted productivity between 14% and 59% on average for real work activities in customer service, writing and programming. The technology appears especially beneficial for less proficient users, helping distribute institutional knowledge. Expert performers gain little because AI cannot surpass human skills refined over years.

While promising, limitations exist. Some users reported generative AI lacked domain-specific expertise to assist fully in niche tasks. Over-reliance on its outputs could also inhibit learning. Nonetheless, the empirical data makes a compelling case that generative AI can enhance productivity if deployed judiciously.

Broader Organizational Impacts

Beyond direct productivity metrics, the same researchers have also investigated generative AI's effects on other workplace outcomes with key findings as follows:

Worker satisfaction: In customer service, agents with access to the AI had improved work satisfaction, driven by greater success handling inquiries. But satisfaction could decline if employees feel generative AI encroaches on their skills and autonomy.

Training: Agents improved faster early in their tenure when using generative AI, reaching expert performance levels quicker. This indicates it may accelerate skill development, an important benefit given constant churn in the labor force.

Soft skills: In customer service, the AI boosted consumer satisfaction by guiding more empathetic responses. This demonstrates generative AI's promise for building emotional intelligence and "people skills."

Consumer perceptions: Consumers gave identical scores to agents with and without the AI, suggesting transparent use of generative AI need not harm customer perceptions if the output quality remains high. But misuse could quickly erode trust.

Inequality: Less skilled workers gained disproportionately across multiple studies. If applied equitably, generative AI could help address income and opportunity disparities stemming from unequal access to training.

These findings show generative AI's multidimensional impacts. While boosting efficiency metrics, integration must also consider effects on corporate culture, employee sentiment, consumer trust, and fair access. A narrowly focused productivity lens could overlook important human issues.

Implementation Challenges

Despite its advantages, effectively leveraging generative AI poses challenges requiring mitigation:

Over-reliance: Users risk over-depending on generative AI outputs without the critical thinking to identify mistakes. This undermines the benefits of human-AI collaboration. Training should highlight the technology's limitations.

De-skilling: Workforce skills could atrophy if generative AI excessively substitutes human capabilities rather than augmenting them. But this appears less concerning since the empirical studies found productivity improvements without full automation.

Security: Cybersecurity vulnerabilities could emerge by relying on generative AI, including model hacking and misuse of sensitive data used in training. Companies must ensure robust protections are in place.

Bias: Due to imperfections in training data, generative AI risks perpetuating harmful biases. Continual monitoring, testing, and refinement of models is necessary to minimize unfair outputs.

Compliance: Generative AI may generate content violating laws or regulations if underlying systems lack oversight. This necessitates human-in-the-loop checks tailored to each use case's risks.

Acceptance: Employees may resist adoption out of unfounded fears of job loss, emphasizing the need for organizational change management and training programs.

Productivity focus: An excessive focus on efficiency metrics could cause firms to overlook generative AI's cultural and ethical implications in areas like employee satisfaction and consumer relationships.

By proactively addressing these areas, companies can maximize productivity gains while safeguarding corporate and stakeholder interests.

Realizing Generative AI's Potential - Recommendations for Business Leaders

The research synthesized in this chapter provides some evidence that generative AI can improve worker productivity, satisfaction, and skill development when thoughtfully deployed. However, adopting these tools involves more than just purchasing and deploying the latest shiny new model. To realize the full benefits, business leaders should consider several recommendations:

Start with focused pilots:

Before attempting wide-scale deployment, pilot generative AI in a few specific use cases where it can clearly enhance productivity based on workflow analysis. Select contained scenarios that limit risks during initial testing. Gather lessons from the pilots before considering larger rollouts to identify optimal integration strategies and change management approaches. Starting small also allows building internal capabilities and comfort with the technology.

Evaluate impacts holistically:

Look beyond productivity metrics alone to fully grasp generative AI's implications. Thoroughly assess its effects on job satisfaction, skill development, equality of access, consumer trust, legal and regulatory compliance, company culture and other outcomes. This holistic perspective ensures you balance productivity objectives with broader ethical and human considerations.

Customize training programs:

Training is critical so employees can maximize generative AI's advantages while avoiding pitfalls like over-reliance. Take care to tailor programs to your organization's specific workflows and use cases, rather than using generic, one-size-fits-all content. Personalized training demonstrates the value proposition to your workers while building their capabilities with your particular AI systems.

Plan for transparency:

Transparency builds trust in AI. But it's not enough to just disclose that generative AI is used. Ensure the systems' behaviors and outputs are transparent as well, providing explainability so any problems can be diagnosed and addressed. Define processes for transparency upfront as part of your integration strategy.

Enable hybrid workflows:

Avoid fully automating tasks with generative AI, as this deprives staff of skill development and oversight. Instead, integrate the technology seamlessly into activities and workflows to foster effective human-AI collaboration. Design interfaces facilitating this hybrid approach.

Continuously monitor for risks:

Due to generative AI's rapid pace of evolution, continuously monitor your systems for potential biases, security vulnerabilities, loss of model integrity over time, and other emerging risks. Establish rigorous oversight processes to identify issues early before they create organizational exposure. Being proactive is essential.

Focus on employee empathy:

Generative AI represents a major change for potentially impacted employees. Go beyond just mandating adoption— take extensive efforts to understand worker perspectives and concerns. Demonstrate the benefits while providing support programs to smooth the transition. Lead with empathy.

The studies reviewed in this chapter confirm that generative AI holds the potential to reshape knowledge work. However, thoughtless application risks severing generative AI's advantages from its drawbacks. By crafting nuanced integration strategies, business leaders can charter a course to generative AI-enhanced productivity, innovation and growth built on a solid ethical and security foundation.

7

THE PERILS OF AUTOMATION

Automation conjures visions of extraordinary capabilities multiplying human potential. As algorithms master activities demanding flexibility and judgment, automation's possibilities seem boundless. Naturally, leaders feel compelled to adopt aggressively this rapidly advancing technology across operations. But in their haste to realize benefits, organizations risk glossing over the immense challenges of integrating automation alongside people. Clumsily implemented, even the most powerful algorithms can degrade team performance, sow friction, and erode that quintessentially human spark.

In this chapter, I distill insights from research to smooth automation adoption. While the research is not focused specifically on generative AI, it provides clues on risks business leaders must actively manage.

When consciously embraced, algorithms still hold potential to enhance productivity without diminishing human strengths. But absent deliberate precautions, even the most advanced AI risks impairing group work, oversight, motivation, and more. By approaching automation's opportunities with eyes wide open to its risks, leaders can avoid its perils.

The Insidious Risks of Automation Blindness

Automation promises to execute certain tasks with super-human speed and precision. But its brittle limitations reveal themselves when the unexpected arises. Studies consistently show that, as overseers, humans make for fickle partners to algorithms. Charged with monitoring for rare failures, boredom and passivity render human supervision unreliable.

This dangerous phenomenon is called automation blindness. When systems rarely misstep during normal operations, humans readily slip into mindless spectating rather than active oversight. Any distractions or complex parallel activities only worsen inattention—divided focus breeds automation complacency. And if people presume systems are highly capable, blindness compounds further. Over-trust leaves people even less likely to notice problems. Facing ambiguous situations, humans defer reflexively to the machine rather than exert effort to think independently.

Decades old experiments dramatize people's elastic tolerance for absurd automation errors. In one study[25], participants failed to react when an AI narrating a children's story made blatantly wrong counting mistakes nearly 30% of the time. Even for such obviously faulty automation, the suspension of disbelief proved enduring. The desire to save attention spans leads people to grant algorithms the benefit of the doubt.

At first glance, such blind faith seems an artifact of laboratory studies. But investigations[26] into disasters like the 2009 Air France Flight 447 crash tell similar tales. The autopilot smoothly handled normal cruising until thunderstorms struck. Then bewildered pilots, struggling to retake control, utterly failed to monitor basic gauges as the aircraft plunged into the Atlantic. Catastrophic blindness is no mere academic curiosity.

The root cause is less about technical capabilities than the unreliable nature of human attention. Optimal collaboration requires keeping humans in the loop—engaged skeptically, not passively along for the ride. Research points to interventions that promote engagement over blind faith:

1. Interacting with the internal reasoning behind AI decisions makes faults more apparent than just showing outputs.
2. Visualizing algorithms' confidence levels fosters healthy skepticism. Uncertainty cues greater vigilance.
3. Regularly prompting humans to acknowledge automation actions keeps them alert through active confirmation.
4. Eliminating competing tasks preserves human focus for oversight duties.
5. Training should stress proactive checking of automation rather than passive reliance on it.

The key is maintaining human agency, not abdicating decisions reflexively to algorithms.

The Hidden Costs of Overly Capable Automation

Many presume that integrating more advanced automation will directly translate into productivity gains. But research reveals that lower-performing algorithms often elicit greater human effort and diligence. When automation makes obvious mistakes, people stay attentive to compensate. Yet flawless performance prompts blind reliance, causing costly disengagement. Workers overly dependent on accurate automation sleepwalk through responsibilities rather than apply their own judgment.

In one recent study[27], researchers asked seasoned HR professionals to review job candidates. Some were paired with highly accurate (85%) AI, others with less accurate (75%) AI, and a control group worked unaided. Contrary to expectations, those with more accurate AI performed worse at identifying strong applicants. The 75% accurate AI increased callbacks 3.4% over human-only teams. But the 85% accurate automation reduced selections 1.2%, underperforming even unaided evaluators.

The data revealed why. Recruiters using more accurate AI spent less time reviewing resumes and gathered less information before deciding. Rather than scrutinizing candidates, they reflexively deferred to the high-performing algorithm. But coupled with marginal human diligence, even imperfect automation boosted overall outcomes. Conversely, nearly flawless algorithms induced passivity, as people discounted their own discernment.

This effect was most pronounced among seasoned recruiters. Veteran evaluators performed worse with highly accurate AI compared to new hires. But their expertise proved valuable in enhancing the less accurate algorithm's suggestions when given room to exercise human judgment. Highly skilled practitioners default to autopilot when automation seems fail-proof. But allowing them to peek under the AI's hood reveals their discernment.

These lessons apply widely:

1. Don't presume more accurate AI is necessarily better. It risks reducing human attentiveness.
2. Consider using less accurate automation in some cases. Imperfect algorithms keep people engaged.
3. Customize automation to user skill levels. Novices may benefit most from highly accurate AI.
4. Incentivize human discretion over blind AI allegiance. Reward those who balance both thoughtfully.
5. Monitor human effort for declines, potentially showing over-reliance on automation.

The key is ensuring algorithms augment, not replace human capabilities. Even high-performing automation benefits from oversight as a corrective against bias and errors. With the right balance, AI can enhance productivity without diminishing hard-won human discernment. But uncritically maximizing automation performance risks complacency and the atrophying of judgment—our last line of defense.

When Automation Disrupts Teamwork

Many technologies that augment individual productivity prove counterproductive for collaborative group work. Take automation. Research shows that injecting algorithms into cooperative activities often hampers performance despite improving individual outputs. Even if automation executes assigned tasks flawlessly, it still destabilizes the collective fabric, enabling smooth coordination.

In one study[28], humans cooperated in a game requiring gathering resources while working in groups of four split into pairs. Midway through games, some pairs had one player swapped with an AI bot. Although these bots individually collected more resources than humans, their presence degraded group-level returns. Human-only teams gathered 15% more resources than joint human-bot teams.

This exposes automation's dark side. AI relentlessly optimized discrete assignments based on narrow algorithms without regard for broader coordination needs. But humans spontaneously adapted to each other's quirks through subtle cues, compensating for miscommunications. Introducing bots disrupted these graceful coordinating rhythms between people.

Beyond raw productivity data, automation also affected psychological dynamics. People reported diminished motivation and engagement after being paired with bots rather than human partners. The impersonal machines corroded intrinsic rewards from cooperating with fellow humans. With automation, the quality of experience suffered even if hard numerical outputs temporarily improved.

These effects held across skill levels. Even top performers struggled to mesh with algorithmic teammates modeled on idealized strategies rather than natural human adaptability. Only rare individuals could still collaborate fluidly amid these disruptions. This highlights automation's immense potential to strain teamwork, even if competence at assigned activities rises.

Reintegrating automation into group workflows ultimately requires a holistic restructuring of team interplay, skill building, and social engineering. Leaders hoping to minimize friction should:

1. Avoid overestimating automation's ability to enhance team collaboration seamlessly. Algorithms can degrade critical coordinating mechanisms.
2. Closely monitor groups for early warning signs of declining motivation, trust, or performance after automation integration.
3. Build in buffers, giving teams time to adapt established processes to account for algorithmic collaborators.
4. Customize training to help individuals interact with automation more effectively based on their roles and capabilities.
5. Engineer automation to support, not constrain, fluid human coordination.
6. Look beyond narrow productivity metrics to gauge automation's impact on qualitative team dimensions.

With thoughtful implementation, organizations may still realize hybrid teams exceeding the sum of their human and algorithmic parts. But crudely substituting automation for people often impairs the bonds that make groups greater than individuals. Renewing those bonds in a new technological era remains automation's central challenge.

The Hidden Risks of Social Loafing in Teams

Most assume collaboration improves results by drawing on diverse strengths. But team settings can also enable social loafing—people exerting less effort while relying on others to pick up the slack. This poses organizations relying on redundancy automation monitoring with a catch-22. Redundant operators are supposed to increase reliability through collective oversight. But diffuse responsibilities often foster complacency, undermining diligence.

Research[33] on redundant automation monitoring exposed this risk. In two studies, investigators compared how two-person teams versus solo operators monitored simulated systems. In both cases, redundant team members performed fewer cross-checks and detected fewer errors compared to solo performers. Working collectively gave people license to loaf, relying on their ostensible partner to catch failures.

This occurs because in groups, people feel their individual contribution matters less to overall outcomes. So they relax their diligence, assuming their partner has things covered. But if both partners loaf to some degree, collective performance suffers rather than improves through pooled oversight. In some cases, even two loafing collaborators failed to match one focused solo operator.

Redundant monitoring proved counterproductive, with combined team vigilance sometimes worse than a single attentive operator. However, simple interventions like feedback on individual performance boosted redundancy's reliability. When contributions remained identifiable despite collaboration, social loafing diminished. People given credit for their own diligence had less incentive to freeload off others.

These findings have implications for leaders in any domain relying on redundancy:

1. Don't assume redundancy ensures reliability. Diffuse responsibilities can reduce diligence.
2. Consider relieving individual burdens rather than ineffective backup. Sometimes, improving solo performance obviates redundancy needs.
3. Ensure individual contributions remain identifiable even within teams. Make autonomy and accountability clear.

Well-designed teams with targeted incentives can still multiply individual diligence through collaboration.

Strategies for Successful Automation Adoption

Harnessing automation's upside while mitigating its down-sides hinges on nuanced implementation. Through deliberate planning, redesign, and skill building, organizations can still benefit from algorithmic augmentation. But simply injecting automation risks degrading teamwork, oversight, and human judgment—which should remain every organization's last line of defense. Avoiding these pitfalls demands approaching integration consciously, proactively, and holistically.

The strategies below aim to smooth automation adoption by steering clear of unintended consequences.

Guard against blind spots:

Promote greater human engagement, skepticism, and attentiveness when interacting with AI systems. Establish oversight protocols, minimizing passive over-reliance and blind deference to algorithms. Design interfaces highlighting uncertainty to cue user vigilance.

Customize rigorously:

Carefully tailor the capabilities and transparency of automation to differences in user expertise, roles, and specific tasks. Seek optimal challenge levels, not maximum autonomy. Novice users may benefit most from highly accurate automation, while experts need transparency to apply their judgment.

Engineer for coordination:

Prioritize system designs and algorithms supporting fluid teamwork over rigid individual optimization. Ensure automation enhances, not disrupts, collaborative rhythms. Recognize that collective performance exceeds the sum of individual outputs.

Motivate discretion:

Provide incentives or recognition for judiciously balancing automation with human judgment and oversight. Avoid undue reliance on algorithms alone or disregard for their capabilities. Reward those who synthesize both thoughtfully.

Monitor impacts closely:

Track early indicators of coordination breakdowns, eroding motivation, disengagement, de-skilling, and other issues resulting from integration struggles. Continually assess effects on qualitative social factors, not just productivity metrics.

Build socio-emotional capacities:

Invest in relationship building, communication, emotional intelligence and other intrinsically human skills to maintain unique strengths alongside automation. Don't focus narrowly on technical prowess alone.

8

THE GENERATIVE AI VALUE CHAIN

Generative AI promises immense opportunities to augment human capabilities across creative expression, knowledge access, productivity, and beyond. Tech visionaries foresee revolutionary transformations paralleling or exceeding prior breakthroughs like electricity, computing, and the internet. However, prudent perspectives understand achieving such grand potential relies on navigating immense complexity across interconnected technological and social dimensions.

This chapter will analyze key components, players, trends, and strategic considerations across the generative AI value chain.

Key Components of the Value Chain

The examples provided in this book aim to bring to life each component of the value chain. They are not vetted business referrals, but examples to broaden business leaders' perspective on how old players are evolving and new players are emerging to serve this new growing area of interest.

A. Data Providers

Training data constitutes the raw material underpinning generative AI capabilities. Scalability demands aggregating corpora spanning billions of examples. Prominent data suppliers include companies like Appen, a leading provider of datasets for machine learning applications across modalities like text, speech, and images. Appen maintains a crowd-sourced base of over 1 million contractors worldwide, providing data annotation services.

The explosive growth in training data demands from state-of-the-art generative models raises several pivotal ethical concerns, warranting proactive mitigation:

- **Representation Bias:** Most available datasets show imbalanced representation across demographic groups that propagate biases absent careful remediation. Thoughtful diversity audits and balancing techniques are essential but challenging to implement at scale.

- **Privacy and Consent:** Rigorously vetting data sources to ensure informed consent and proper rights is imperative, particularly for any personal information. Many public datasets likely violate reasonable expectations.

- **Misuse:** Generative models amplify any toxicity or misinformation present in training data. Malicious actors could also deliberately poison datasets in

attempts to manipulate outputs. Ongoing
monitoring is prudent.

- **Environmental:** The computational demands of
  processing massive datasets carries non-trivial
  carbon footprints often overlooked. Optimizing
  data reuse provides partial mitigation.

As algorithms scale in capability, so too must diligent oversight of associated training data inputs to uphold ethical development. Establishing sound datasets requires significant investments, paralleling the technical challenges of model development.

B. Computer Hardware

Specialized parallel processors like GPUs and TPUs provide the massively distributed computing vital for developing and running advanced neural network models.

NVIDIA dominates the GPU market optimized for deep learning workloads. Its A100 can perform up to 20 quadrillion operations per second to power next-generation AI applications. Cloud vendors offer remote access to clusters of hundreds of cutting-edge GPUs and TPUs for organizations lacking sufficient own data center resources. Specialized AI accelerators for edge and endpoint deployment are also emerging, including those from startups like Synthesis AI.

We will explore generative AI's computational power demands and ecosystem more deeply in the next chapter.

C. Cloud Platforms

Leading cloud vendors offer tailored services powering key steps across the generative AI value chain:

- Google Cloud Platform: Provides TensorFlow-optimized TPUs, scalable model training/serving, pre-built AI building blocks, and other machine learning (ML) focused tooling. Leverages Google's strengths in proprietary models, research, and talent.

- AWS: Leads in provisioning GPUs for training complex models. SageMaker enables no-code model building, hyper-parameter tuning, and deployment. These are tightly integrated with other AWS offerings.

- Microsoft Azure: State-of-the-art machine learning capabilities deeply interwoven with Microsoft's substantial software ecosystem. Azure OpenAI service provides access to GPT-3 API.

- NVIDIA NGC: Specialized cloud platform optimized for AI featuring NVIDIA's latest GPUs and reference architectures for accelerating workflow pipelines.

- Databricks: Specializes in data engineering, model training acceleration, MLOps, and other steps in the generative AI value chain. Uses open source foundations augmented with proprietary value-adds.

Multi-cloud strategies provide flexibility and mitigate risks of over-reliance on any single vendor. However, switching costs remain high once invested. Maintaining some on-premise infrastructure warrants consideration alongside cloud services. Mindful design maximizes strengths while minimizing pitfalls.

D. Foundation Models

Specialized firms and labs, like OpenAI, develop and release pre-trained models constituting the algorithmic foundations upon which downstream applications are constructed. Let's explore a few others:

- Anthropic: Pioneering techniques like Constitutional AI to align models with human values. Its Claude model aims for broad capabilities with robust safeties.

- Cohere: Focused on developing fast, lightweight, and affordable NLP models for enterprise applications.

Careful evaluation of model pedigree, capabilities, limitations, and ethical alignment is imperative before integration. Tuning foundations for specific needs through transfer learning often proves more effective than training custom models from scratch. We will explore this later in the book.

E. Model Hubs and MLOps

Model hubs and machine learning operations (MLOps) platforms facilitate efficiently leveraging foundation models. Hugging Face Hub, for example, enables discovering, evaluating, and integrating over 30,000 community-uploaded models for fine-tuning. Handles versioning and model sharing.

Widely adopted MLOps platforms streamline development while upholding oversight throughout the machine learning lifecycle. However, sole reliance on external proprietary systems poses risks of lock-in inhibiting flexibility. Maintaining in-house integration expertise provides independence while leveraging partnerships judiciously.

F. Applications

Generative AI enables a proliferating array of applications demoing remarkable versatility:

- Chatbots: Provide conversational customer service, sales, and support via natural language interactions. Leading vendors include Anthropic, Cohere, and Google's Dialogflow.

- Content Creation: Generate marketing copy, reports, code, and other materials customized on demand. Companies like Jasper and Novel AI offer specialized writing aids.

- Process Automation: Produce data summaries, analysis, insights, and structured information tailored to business workflows.

- Translation: Convert between languages while preserving nuance.

G. Services

Professional services support customizing, applying, and scaling generative AI capabilities:

- Data Services: Procure, prepare, label, augment, and verify training data.

- Model Services: Tailor, train, optimize, and audit models based on business needs and ethical considerations.

- Prompt Engineering: Refine models for specialized applications and domains via prompting strategies.

- MLOps Services: Productionize models at scale, including robust deployment, monitoring, maintenance, and updates.

- Strategy Consulting: Guide direction and adoption planning for generative AI across operations.

Carefully balancing internal skills cultivation with external partnerships proves prudent for most organizations. However, many still under-invest in developing requisite in-house competencies, posing risks.

Emerging Trends Reshaping the AI Ecosystem

The generative AI landscape continues rapidly evolving across all components of the value chain. Several pivotal developments are disrupting historic patterns:

I. Right-sized Models:

Massive models with hundreds of billions of parameters or more prove unnecessary for many business applications. New techniques enable matches to large foundation capabilities with 10-100x fewer parameters, reducing costs and resources dramatically. We will review these techniques in more detail in later chapters.

2. Specialized Data:

Curated datasets narrowly tailored for industry verticals and individual companies appear superior to reliance purely on the broadest corpora scraped non-consensually from the web.

3. Responsible Scaling Mindsets:

Thoughtless pursuit of scale absent ethics risks amplifying dangers via generative models. Maintaining human oversight, representative data/teams, testing, and alignment incentives helps ensure responsible development. But collective action is imperative for preserving diligence amidst exponential trends.

4. Democratized Access:

Walled gardens around proprietary models inhibit innovation. Open ecosystems for cooperative model development like Hugging Face's community aim to circumvent this through radical collaboration and transparency. User-funded models promise reduced reliance on surveillance and targeted advertising.

4. Edge Capabilities:

Performing inference directly on devices like smartphones, Internet of Things (IoT) sensors, and edge networks provides several benefits compared to relying on the cloud.

It keeps data and computations localized on-device avoids sending sensitive user data to the cloud, which could expose it to hacking or surveillance. This increases privacy.

On-device inference avoids round-trip delays communicating with cloud servers which can introduce lag, especially for real-time applications like augmented reality. Processing locally reduces latency.

Additionally, devices can still perform inference even with poor internet connectivity or if cloud services go down. This makes applications more robust and reliable. No cloud usage for inference computations also reduces operational costs, especially at scale. Energy-efficient on-device inference chips further reduce costs.

To enable on-device inference, optimized software frameworks like Tensorflow Lite Micro and PyTorch Mobile allow compressing and deploying neural network models on resource-constrained devices. They provide optimizations like quantization, pruning, and efficient kernels specialized for mobile/embedded deployment.

Some startups, like Synthesis AI focus specifically on model compression techniques to make large state-of-the-art models viable on edge devices. Their solutions promise high accuracy while meeting tight resource constraints.

Key Implications for Business Leaders

Navigating generative AI's value chain strategically constitutes an imperative and complex challenge amidst exponential technological change. Recommendations for harnessing possibilities while addressing risks responsibly include:

1. Audit Data and Models Rigorously

Scrutinize training data composition and possible biases extensively. Rigorously test models for safety issues like toxicity across representative groups. Enable continuous feedback channels conveying concerns. Lacking transparency creates blind spots threatening unintended harm. Institute and operationalize responsible data practices.

2. Maintain Flexibility in Infrastructure

Avoid over-reliance on specific providers. Manage sensitivity to vendor lock-in when choosing cloud platforms. Nurture optionality to pivot across offerings as competitive dynamics shift. Experiment judiciously with on-premise and edge capabilities, balancing strengths appropriately.

3. Balance Internal Skill Development with Partnerships

Carefully cultivate in-house competencies in key areas like data curation, prompt engineering, and MLOps while also leveraging specialized external providers strategically. Avoid calcified frameworks stifling necessary flexibility. Focus investments on sustainable differentiating capabilities.

4. Evaluate Integration Requirements Rigorously

Realizing value requires seamless enterprise integration. Assess gaps in current infrastructure capabilities, prompting interfaces, workflows, monitoring needs, and maintenance processes. Well-designed integration maximizes utility while minimizing disruption. Plan iterations leveraging continuous user feedback.

9

THE STAGGERING COMPUTATIONAL POWER BEHIND GENERATIVE AI

Generative AI has captured the world's attention with applications like chatbots and image generation. But what's hidden from view is the staggering amount of computational power required to make these systems work. For non-technical business leaders, it's difficult to fully grasp the scale of computation involved. This chapter aims to break it down in simple terms by exploring:

1. The specialized hardware driving neural networks.
2. The skyrocketing demand and costs for AI compute.
3. Strategies small business are using to compete against big tech firms.
4. What the future may hold as algorithms, data, and hardware evolve.

Understanding these forces is key for business leaders making decisions in the generative AI space. While the computational requirements seem daunting, democratization may come through better algorithms, strategic data, innovative model training strategies, and emerging hardware.

GPUs: The Specialized Engine Behind Neural Networks

Let's start by understanding what hardware makes generative AI possible in the first place. While early neural networks ran on normal computer processors (CPUs), today's systems are powered by graphical processing units (GPUs). Originally designed for rendering video game graphics, GPUs excel at parallel processing—doing many calculations simultaneously.

This capability is crucial because neural networks rely on processing huge matrices of numbers in parallel. A core building block of neural networks is the matrix multiplication operation. GPUs can multiply two matrices in a single operation by assigning each element-wise multiplication to a separate processing core. With thousands of cores, they handle matrices efficiently.

By contrast, CPUs were designed to execute programs line by line. While modern CPUs include multiple cores to allow some parallelization, GPUs take parallel processing to the extreme. Top-end GPUs today, like the Nvidia A100, contain over 54 billion transistors, allowing up to 312 multiplications per cycle.

To appreciate why GPU acceleration is so important, let's examine GPT-3. It requires a ballpark of over 300 billion floating point operations just for a single inference, like when it responds to a prompt! Without GPU acceleration, using just CPUs, it would take months rather than milliseconds to process an input and generate an output. The massive parallelization of GPUs unlocks the computational speed needed.

The same is true for training these models, which requires even more intensive mathematics as the system learns from data. Training GPT-3 is estimated to have required over 10^23 floating point operations in total—that's a number with 23 zeros after it! Only massively parallel GPUs clustered together can handle this scale of computation in any reasonable timeframe. This results in an estimated carbon footprint of over 626,000 pounds—nearly 5 times the emissions of the average American car's lifetime.[38]

Also, research suggests that training GPT-3 in Microsoft's U.S. data centers:

> can directly consume 700,000 liters of clean freshwater, enough for producing 370 BMW cars or 320 Tesla electric vehicles, and these numbers would have been tripled if GPT-3 were trained in Microsoft's Asian data centers.
>
> —Pengfei Li, Jianyi Yang, et al.[39]

Nvidia's pioneering efforts have cemented its position as the leading GPU manufacturer for AI applications. Yet, the race is far from over. Companies like Intel and AMD, along with cloud giants like Amazon and Google, are launching their custom chips, such as Tensor Processing Units (TPUs) to capture a slice of the AI hardware pie.

However, GPUs designed for gaming and graphics still form the backbone of most AI systems today. Their adaptability to matrix math and ability to pack in thousands of parallel cores has made them the workhorse driving the AI revolution. So while GPUs were originally built just to render video game environments, their unique architecture turned out to be perfectly suited to powering neural networks.

Skyrocketing Demand for Compute

But supply of these AI-optimized GPUs is not keeping up with demand. In fact, by some estimates, demand for AI hardware outstrips supply by 10x. The AI boom caught much of the technology industry off guard with its sudden explosion in popularity. Chip fabrication plants, known as "fabs", take billions of dollars and years to build.

You can't just press a button and build 10X more.

—Robert Ober, Nvidia[34]

AI demand has grown much faster than new manufacturing capabilities can be brought online. Established fabs are stretched to their limits fulfilling orders from Big Tech giants like Google, Amazon, Meta, and Microsoft, who are all racing to deploy AI internally and in consumer products. This is creating a crunch for startups and smaller players seeking access to GPUs or other AI hardware.

The core issue is that running state-of-the-art generative AI requires immense amounts of parallel processing power. As AI models grow ever larger and more ambitious, their hunger for computing resources scales exponentially.

For example, as previously discussed, GPT-3 has approximately 175 billion parameters, while the successor GPT-4 is rumored to have over 1 trillion parameters—a more than 5x increase. This has led to a gold rush dynamic where scarce GPU access goes to the highest bidder.

Businesses are being forced to make multi-year commitments to cloud vendors just to get basic access to a handful of GPUs or TPUs. In some cases, tech giants will make direct investments in promising startups to guarantee them privileged access to chips coming off the manufacturing lines.

For any company pursuing generative AI, the cost of compute can quickly become the single largest expense. Some startups are spending 80% of capital raised on securing compute access. In essence, they need to choose between using those dollars for hiring more team members or deploying larger models. This tradeoff is slowing AI innovation and putting startups at a disadvantage compared to big tech firms.

Analyzing the Cost to Train a Model like GPT-3

Let's examine the specific costs involved in developing generative AI models, starting with model training. This is the expensive and computationally intensive process of actually creating the AI algorithm based on analyzing huge datasets.

As previously discussed, state-of-the-art natural language models like GPT-3 are known as transformer models. They comprise multiple layers with billions of adjustable parameters that must be carefully tuned during the training process. The cost to train one of these models can run into the millions of dollars, with some estimates north of $10 million for GPT-3.

To understand why, we need to grasp the sheer scale of computation required. Let's take GPT-3 as a concrete example. It uses 175 billion parameters that must be tuned over the course of training on over a trillion tokens of text data.

Remember that a token is a piece of data like a word or a byte. So a trillion tokens equates to terabytes of textual data from sources like books, Wikipedia, websites, and more. Each of the 175 billion parameters requires multiple floating point operations to adjust and tune it correctly based on this training data.

When you multiply 175 billion by the multiple floating point operations per parameter and then by a trillion tokens, it leads to a total computation requirement on the order of 10^{23} operations. This is an almost incomprehensible scale of computation.

To put it in perspective, if every person on earth did one billion operations per second, it would take over 6 months for the global population to complete what GPT-3 required. This helps drive home why specialized hardware like GPUs with massively parallel capabilities is an absolute necessity.

And remember that the model must be trained repeatedly as new data becomes available. There is no such thing as a one-time training cost for an AI system if you want it to stay relevant and capable. Every update requires running through the iterative optimization process across all parameters on the latest datasets.

Additionally, there are all the failed experimental runs that accumulate costs. AI research involves constant experimentation with model architectures, hyper-parameters, and training techniques. Many of those experiments fail and have to be re-run. When you factor in the need to reserve GPU capacity months in advance, the total training bill for a model like GPT-3 comes out to tens of millions of dollars.

And that's just for specialized natural language models. For computer vision models that generate images and videos, the costs are even higher due to larger model sizes and more expensive data labeling requirements.

Analyzing the Cost of Running AI Inference

As previously discussed, once an AI model like GPT-3 is fully trained, delivering it to users is called inference. This requires exponentially fewer computations since the model's billions of parameters are already tuned and established. But inference still carries a significant cost, especially if you want to provide responsive, uninterrupted service.

The expense stems primarily from the provisioning capacity for usage spikes and redundancy. Let's suppose we are running a conversational chatbot powered by GPT-3. If the service faces a 10x demand surge on Monday mornings as people chat with the bot over their morning coffee, you need to pay for having 10x capacity sitting idle late on Saturday nights when usage drops.

Plus, you need redundancy across geographic regions and backup servers in case of outages. If an Amazon data center goes down, you can't afford your chatbot experiencing any hiccups. So you pay 2x for full redundancy. When you factor in all of these realities, inference can still cost a meaningful amount, even if per-query costs are negligible.

Unlike training, the inference costs are directly proportional to user traffic. If your product takes off, as you hope it will, inference requirements spike up with it. This can make cost unpredictable and requires careful capacity planning. Techniques like load testing, auto-scaling, and optimizing latency are key.

Additionally, not all inferences are created equal. A quick chat response can be handled by an AI assistant on someone's smartphone. But a complex multi-step question may need to tap into a beefier inference server with greater capabilities. Striking the right balance between on-device versus cloud-based inference is an art and science.

The good news is that, once trained, generative AI models can be applied in myriad ways through inference. The same model can power a website chatbot, a conversational app on smartphones, a voice assistant device and more. Amortizing training costs across different applications and use cases is important for achieving return on investment.

The AI Compute Arms Race

We've established that developing cutting edge foundational models requires prohibitive amounts of compute resources. This presents a challenge for new entrants since big tech firms have an inherent advantage. They can marshal more dollars, data scientists, and proprietary datasets to produce ever larger and more capable models.

In an environment where model size and training data quantity correlate closely with capability, this results in something of an AI compute arms race. Small businesses and academics simply can't compete with the resources that giants like Google, Meta, and Microsoft can pour into developing new AI algorithms. The AI compute arms race increasingly looks like a winner-take-all environment where the biggest players seize the largest market share. Examples of big tech firms taking control over the generative AI ecosystem include Microsoft's stake in OpenAI, and the most recent $235 million capital investment round on Hugging Face by Salesforce, NVIDIA, Google, and Amazon. Hugging Face is most recognized for its transformers model library, and its platform that enables users to share models and datasets.

Strategies to Compete Against Big Tech Firms

However, alternatives are emerging to help smaller players compete against tech giants in the generative AI race. One approach focuses on developing models with a more limited scope but extremely high capability within that domain.

By focusing on a narrowly defined use case, it's possible to train capable models with orders of magnitude fewer data than systems designed to be general purpose conversationalists like GPT-3.

Businesses are also innovating with architectures that connect smaller modules into an ensemble system. This allows mixing and matching sets of skills based on user needs. For example, a scientific question answering module could be combined with a module specialized in mathematical reasoning. Modules with millions rather millions of billions of parameters may be sufficient and avoid computational bottlenecks.

Emerging techniques for parameter-efficient fine-tuning (PEFT)[35] [36] of pre-trained models like Low-Rank Adaptation (LoRA)[37] are a great alternative for those leveraging existing base models.

Plus, innovative hardware initiatives hold promise to deliver better efficiency margins for training.

So while compute scale remains a daunting barrier, there are rays of light for new players. Democratization may come through better algorithms, PEFT, strategic training data, and specialized hardware. But computational power remains imperative to realizing the full possibilities of generative AI. Understanding these technology tradeoffs is key for business leaders making decisions in this emerging ecosystem.

The Road Ahead: Where AI Compute Costs Are Headed

Looking to the future, the demand for AI compute power will likely continue rising, but the outlook for costs is more uncertain. On the supply side, chip fabrication plants take years to build, so supply will remain constrained in the short term. Cloud providers are racing to add capacity, but their larger enterprise customers get priority.

However, if supply eventually catches up with demand, it could drive down costs. Some experts[30] believe we are near the limits of training dataset scale, suggesting model size may plateau. If model size flattens while GPU performance continues increasing per Moore's Law, it could bend the cost curve. But new unforeseen model architectures could drive costs back up.

On the demand side, the broader adoption of AI across industries will fuel surging compute needs, even if model size stabilizes. Every company will be experimenting with AI, driving up cloud demand. But techniques like reduced precision computing, model pruning, and specialized chips promise improved efficiency.

Ultimately the future of AI compute costs will be driven by the interplay between supply and demand forces. While explosive growth has defined the last few years, bends in the curve that lower costs are likely on the horizon. But the extent and timing remain uncertain. Flexibility and having a strategic approach will be key for businesses navigating this fast-moving landscape.

Key Questions Business Leaders Should Consider

Artificial intelligence promises immense opportunities but also carries new complexities for strategic decision makers. Here are some key questions business leaders should reflect on given the realities revealed in this deep dive:

- What in-house data assets could we leverage to train AI models for our needs responsibly?

- How much control over AI compute resources and proprietary models do we require versus relying on third-party cloud services?

- Are there ways to adopt a more scoped, focused approach to AI that requires less data compute compared to general solutions?

- How can we train models efficiently to minimize sustainability impacts?

- How will we power AI systems through renewable energy and offset emissions?

- How will AI affect our carbon emissions, water usage, and overall ESG goals?

- Where can we use AI to improve our sustainability initiatives in other business areas?

The compute dimensions explored in depth here represent just one piece of the generative AI puzzle. But understanding these forces is crucial for business leaders to make bold decisions navigating the AI revolution. While the computational requirements seem staggering, strategic thinking can open new paths to participate.

Key Takeaways for Business Leaders

- GPUs are the specialized high-performance hardware driving neural network AI thanks to parallel processing capability, but consume immense electricity, demanding renewable energy sourcing.

- Demand for AI compute far outstrips supply, forcing startups to dedicate huge percentages of capital to securing cloud compute access.

- Training cutting-edge generative models like GPT-3 costs upwards of millions of tons of CO_2 emissions, due to the extraordinary computational requirements.

- Running models in production (inference) still carries meaningful costs for provisioning capacity to handle surges and redundancy.

- The AI compute arms race favors large tech firms, but new approaches are emerging to help democratize access to these powerful technologies.

10

THE HIGH-STAKES BATTLE FOR THE FUTURE OF AI: OPEN SOURCE VS. BIG TECH TITANS

P owerful new technologies like large language models have captured public imagination. These models have the potential to transform industries and economies—but could also lead to harmful consolidation if policymakers and business leaders are not proactive.

Unlike previous AI breakthroughs which saw rapid consolidation, competition still appears vibrant. This is due to a few key factors. Many new models are being released with open APIs or as open source, whereas past AI was closely guarded proprietary tech. This promotes third-party innovation. In addition, novel training techniques, like LoRA[37], are allowing smaller players to compete by reducing data and computing requirements.

However, open access can't be taken for granted. General public models like ChatGPT enjoy powerful data network effects that can enable one or two players to achieve runaway dominance. The more users a model has, the more data it accumulates, the faster it improves—attracting even more users. Behind the scenes, technology titans like

Google, Meta, Microsoft, and OpenAI are engaged in a high-stakes battle for dominance and control over the future trajectory of AI.

A 2023 Time cover: "The AI Arms Race Is Changing Everything"[66]

Increasingly, this clash appears to hinge on the competition between open source and proprietary approaches to developing AI systems. Open source AI refers to AI systems built with transparent code and data, available for anyone to use, modify, extend, and build upon freely. This stands in contrast to proprietary AI models controlled by large technology companies as guarded trade secrets. Smaller businesses and startups have an opening thanks to open source foundations and advancing techniques. But long-term viability remains unproven.

OpenAI was once at the forefront of open source principles, starting life as a nonprofit lab in 2015 with the mission to "build value for everyone rather than shareholders" and a policy encouraging employees to "publish their work, whether as papers, blog posts, or code." But in recent years, OpenAI has drifted towards increasingly closed practices, especially after accepting Microsoft's $1 billion investment in 2019. OpenAI has also shifted away from initially vocal concerns about the safety risks of releasing powerful AI systems freely into the world, towards defending and promoting its own models like GPT-3 and GPT-4 for commercial gain, while warning about the dangers of even more advanced alternatives.

Many proponents have positioned open source as the antidote to excessive concentration of power and ownership of AI among a handful of Big Tech corporations like Google, Meta, Microsoft and OpenAI itself. Open systems can enable much broader innovation in AI beyond the restrictive walled gardens of the tech giants, allowing independent researchers, startups, nonprofits, and the public to audit, participate, and build upon AI freely. However, historically, the major technology companies have proven adept at co-opting open source for competitive advantage, integrating open innovations into their proprietary products and services while ceding little ground in their dominance.

Google's Anxiety About Losing Ground to Open Source AI

A recently leaked internal Google memo[31] provides a remarkable window into the company's growing anxiety about losing ground to open source AI systems:

We aren't positioned to win this arms race and neither is OpenAI. While we've been squabbling amongst each other, a third faction has been quietly eating our lunch. I'm talking, of course, about open source.

The memo openly admits Google now trails the open source community badly in generative AI: open source models frequently match or surpass the capabilities of Google's internally developed models, despite requiring vastly lower financial investments and computational resources.

The memo highlights how open systems inherently enable collaboration at a global scale that cannot be matched within the confines of any corporation. As just one example, it describes how thousands of employees at the company Databricks[32] banded together quickly to crowdsource high-quality question-and-answer pairs for an open source model called Dolly over the course of mere weeks. By contrast, Google and OpenAI have relied on scraping forums like Reddit to get their training data. The data behind Dolly comes straight from professionals aiming to produce an information resource of greater depth and quality compared to the typical scraps of conversational data extracted from public internet forums.

The Google memo also warns that sheer model scale and expense, formerly considered one of Google's core advantages, have now transformed into hindrances compared to the relatively nimble pace of innovation demonstrated by the open source community:

Things we consider 'major open problems' are solved and in people's hands today... At the beginning of March the open source community got their hands on their first really capable foundation model [Meta's leaked LLaMA]. A tremendous outpouring of innovation followed, with just days between major developments.

The blinding pace of open source community advances in AI are perhaps most vividly illustrated in the field of image generation. The open source image generation system Stable Diffusion, first released in August 2022, rapidly eclipsed usage of Open AI's DALL-E image AI just weeks after its introduction, according to the memo. This demonstrates the formidable velocity and swarm-like collaborative power embodied by the global open source community that cannot be easily matched by any single corporation.

The Long History of Tech Giants Co-opting Open Source for Competitive Gain

However, the major technology companies have a long history of successfully co-opting open source technologies originally aimed at democratizing access to technology for their own competitive advantage, while often paying lip service to ideals of democratization.

Some companies have moved to embrace 'open' AI as a mechanism to entrench dominance, using the rhetoric of 'open' AI to expand market power while investing in 'open' AI efforts in ways that allow them to set standards of development while benefiting from the free labor of open source contributors.

– David Gray Widder, Sarah West, Meredith Whittaker[64]

Large tech corporations adeptly use their sheer scale and resources to set standards effectively and steer the direction of open source projects in alignment with their own commercial interests, while benefiting tremendously from the free labor contributed by external open source developers to improve their ecosystems.

For instance, Google's TensorFlow and Meta's PyTorch machine learning frameworks are designed to optimize for integration with their respective company's proprietary cloud computing platforms, attracting adherents from researchers and developers who appreciate the convenience of seamless integration.

As Meta CEO Mark Zuckerberg candidly admitted in a recent earnings call, open sourcing PyTorch:

---

integrates with our technology stack, [so] when there are opportunities to make integrations with products, it's much easier to make sure that developers and other folks are compatible with the things that we need in the way that our systems work.

Often, the most significant "open" aspects of "open" AI consist of releasing pre-trained models like Google's BERT and Meta's LLaMA under permissive licenses. These foundation models get outside developers off to a head start by providing a strong basis they can build on top of via techniques like fine-tuning for specific tasks, as opposed to building entirely novel models from scratch.

However, even these open source pre-trained models overwhelmingly continue to run on the Big Tech cloud computing platforms like AWS, Azure and GCP when deployed in practice. Additionally, corporations stand to gain immense an advantage by reintegrating improvements contributed by the open source community back into their own commercial offerings.

True Open Collaboration Requires Infrastructure Independence

The current reality is that fine-tuning Big Tech's open source AI models does not fundamentally constitute decentralization or democratization of AI. True open collaboration and innovation requires freedom and independence—the ability to build from the ground up without reliance on the proprietary stacks and ecosystems controlled by a handful of large technology corporations.

Presently, foundational resources essential to cutting-edge AI research and development like compute power, datasets, development frameworks and pre-trained models, remain overwhelmingly centralized under the control of Amazon, Microsoft, Google and several other giants who operate the dominant cloud computing platforms. Open source efforts cannot truly flourish or compete if trapped within the confines of the Big Tech clouds and proprietary ecosystems.

Policymakers are scrutinizing the immense and still increasing concentration of power and ownership in the AI technology sector. But well-intentioned interventions like regulations and breakups could inadvertently reinforce the dominance of existing centralized infrastructure and ecosystems if not carefully designed—hardly a huge concern for the principal giants in the scheme of their multi-trillion dollar enterprises.

Instead, regulators and lawmakers should promote policies explicitly aimed at nurturing fertile ground for independent open source development to thrive outside the restrictions of proprietary technology stacks operated by megalithic corporate clouds. For instance, governments could fund and support accessible non-corporate super-computing capabilities for training models, sponsor creation of diverse public open datasets, and provide incentives for researchers to build important new AI models from scratch under permissive open licenses, rather than solely relying on fine-tuning Big Tech's existing foundation models.

The future of AI need not devolve into a simplistic false choice between completely untrammeled openness and heavy-handed bans or restrictions driven by overzealous regulation. But we must tread carefully and intentionally to cultivate open, collaborative AI ecosystems that can flourish beyond the walled gardens and tightly controlled proprietary stacks of Big Tech. Only by doing so can we hope to tap into the full potential for transformative innovation promised by AI in a manner that broadly benefits society.

The High-Stakes Battle For Control of the Trajectory of AI

Open source philosophies once promised to democratize access to cutting-edge technologies radically. Yet for AI, the eventual outcome of the high-stakes battle between open and closed systems remains highly uncertain.

Powerful incentives pull major corporate powers to co-opt open source efforts for greater profit and control, however subtly such dynamics might unfold. Yet independent open communities intrinsically chafe against restrictions and centralized control over capacity to innovate. Both sides are digging in for a long fight.

The leaked memo from Google signals the internet giant fears losing control of its once seemingly unassailable lead in AI, as decentralized open systems demonstrate abilities to unlock collaborative potential at global scales impossible within the confines of any single private corporate entity. The battle for the future path of artificial intelligence has only just begun.

The Path Forward for Business Leaders

As the competition between open source and proprietary AI intensifies, business leaders face critical decisions on how to adopt AI capabilities strategically without ceding too much control or becoming locked into restrictive ecosystems. Here is important guidance for navigating this complex landscape:

1. Evaluate risks of provider lock-in and lack of transparency

Relying too heavily on proprietary AI from a single tech giant creates concerning dependencies. Lack of visibility into training data and model logic with closed systems also presents risks. Thoroughly analyze trade-offs of leveraging open source versus commercial providers in terms of transparency, extensibility, and avoidance of lock-in.

2. Explore niche ecosystem models tailored to your needs

Emerging open source communities are creating vibrant ecosystems tailored to specific industries' needs, like medicine or finance. These ecosystems can offer affordable access to high-quality training data, models and tooling customized to your domain. Though smaller in scale than Big Tech clouds, they provide targeted capabilities without lock-in.

3. Invest in internal skills to fine-tune and audit foundation models

Whether using open source or commercial models, having in-house expertise to adapt models and rigorously evaluate outputs instills greater control. Prioritize growing multidisciplinary teams encompassing data science, engineering and ethics to customize, enhance and audit AI responsibly according to your business requirements.

4. Be ready to switch providers if performance stagnates or costs escalate

Avoid over-investing in proprietary ecosystems so you retain flexibility to adopt alternatives. Keep integration modular and data accessible. Contribute to open standards. These measures keep options open if your current vendor relationship sours or open source models pull ahead.

5. Foster partnerships while still owning key IP

Collaborate with researchers and niche providers via contracts granting your business ownership of core novel IP developed on top of models you rightfully licensed. This balances openness to spur innovation with protecting vital differentiators.

6. Get clarity on permissible training data use

Work with legal counsel to develop policies and obtain licenses allowing use of proprietary text, images or other data in model training, subject to appropriate data privacy measures. IP issues loom otherwise, but many opportunities exist for mutually beneficial data sharing.

7. Stay abreast of emerging regulations

Watch especially for new rules regarding required transparency, audits, liability and IP for AI systems as governments catch up with technological realities. Move proactively toward responsible practices that likely will be codified into law.

In summary, avoid over-dependence on restrictive proprietary ecosystems as competition between open and closed
AI intensifies. With strategic foresight and dedication to
developing internal expertise, businesses can responsibly
harness the power of AI without ceding too much control.
Though challenges exist, the incredible potential makes
navigating this complex terrain imperative.

11

THE GENERATIVE AI PROJECT LIFECYCLE

Implementing generative AI requires thoughtful planning and execution spanning model selection, training, integration, and monitoring. This chapter provides an overview of the key phases in a generative AI project lifecycle to serve as a blueprint for leaders exploring this technology. I cover the lifecycle at a high-level, focusing on the why and what of each phase, while leaving details to later chapters.

Lifecycle Overview

1. Define use case:

- Identify business needs
- Frame objectives
- Set success metrics

2. Select base model:

- Pre-trained or custom

- Consider capabilities, speed, cost
- Review platform and tools

3. Adapt model:

- Prompt engineering
- Fine-tuning
- Human feedback loops
- Evaluation

4. Integrate and deploy:

- Optimize for inference
- Develop applications
- Monitoring and compliance

Defining the Use Case

The first step in any generative AI project is identifying a clear business need that this technology can potentially address. As mentioned in previous chapters, some common use cases include conversational agents or content creation.

The use case should be specific enough to guide the model selection and training process but broad enough to allow flexibility in the integration phase. For instance, a business may need an AI assistant to respond to basic customer service queries or want to use generative AI to create fact sheets about their products from templates.

Equally crucial is defining what success looks like even before development begins. Quantifiable metrics could include:

- Reduced time for content creation by 40%.
- Improved quality score for generated text from 3/5 to 4/5.
- 90% accuracy in answering customer questions without escalation.

Such goals align stakeholder expectations and provide concrete yardsticks to evaluate the generative AI application later.

When framing the use case, it is also important to consider broader stakeholder needs through an ethical lens. How will the generative AI impact people within the organization? Does it create re-skilling opportunities or redundancy? Are there concerns around data privacy or copyright infringement that need addressing? What is the carbon footprint and environmental impact?

Taking a human-centric, design thinking approach can shed light on all stakeholder perspectives—employees, customers, local communities, regulators etc. Incorporating such considerations in the use case definition ensures a holistic framing that serves both business objectives and social good.

Selecting the Base Model

Once the use case is established, the next step is selecting an appropriate base model that will be adapted and optimized for the business need. There are a few options:

1. **Pre-trained models:** Most common are foundation models from vendors like Anthropic, Cohere, OpenAI, and AI21 which are trained on huge text corpuses. Popular

examples are Claude 2, GPT-4, Codex, and Jurassic-2. They can generate text responses from short prompts right out of the box.

2. Custom models: For more specialized needs, custom models can be trained from scratch on proprietary datasets though this requires significant time and resources.

When short-listing options, key factors to consider are:

- **Model size:** Larger models (with billions of parameters) are more powerful but slower and costlier for inferences.

- **Training data:** Models trained on diverse, high-quality data handle a wider range of tasks better.

- **Capabilities:** Assess available models on accuracy, reasoning ability, creativity based on test prompts. You may also need to assess domain or use case specific capabilities such as financial language or long-form writing capabilities.

- **Inference speed:** Critical if the AI application is customer-facing with real-time expectations.

- **Cost:** Account for usage-based pricing from vendors as well as compute and engineering resources.

- **Platform and tools:** Evaluate model development platforms, SDKs, APIs provided to integrate, monitor and manage the model post-deployment.

- **Ethical considerations:** Assess sustainability, labor practices and the vendors' ESG commitments.

Leverage smaller models where possible to optimize for cost and speed without compromising on quality.

Adapting the Model

The next phase focuses on customizing the base model for optimal performance on the target use case. There are a few techniques to adapt models:

- **Prompt engineering:** Prompt formulation guides the model's behavior without modifying the actual parameters. Prompts provide context to the model and constrain outputs to match the application needs. For example, a long conversational prompt can get a nuanced dialogue from the model.

- **Fine-tuning:** This involves additional training by exposing the model to custom datasets relevant to the downstream task. For instance, a marketing content generator can be fine-tuned on a client's past ad copies and product catalogs. Fine-tuning significantly boosts the performance of foundation models.

- **Human feedback loops:** Generating sample outputs and manually labeling them as right/wrong provides learning signal for models to continue improving. For example, a product description generator can be further refined based on human ratings.

Evaluation is key during the adaptation phase to quantify progress. Example metrics are similarity to domain-specific text, coherence, grammar, accuracy for classification/extraction tasks, etc. The model should demonstrate solid performance across metrics on test data before integration into applications. Rigorous evaluation also flags any biased or incorrect outputs early.

Application Integration

Once the model development is complete, the final phase focuses on integration and deployment for end-users. Key steps include:

- **Optimizing for inference:** Before deployment, models undergo additional processing to optimize their speed and performance. This includes converting them to efficient formats suitable for apps, websites and devices. Advanced techniques like quantization and pruning are applied. Quantization reduces the precision of model calculations to use less memory and compute power. Pruning removes redundant model connections. Together, these techniques enable real-time, stable predictions on limited computing resources like phones or tablets. Optimization ensures the AI experience is fast and seamless for end-users.

- **Building applications:** LLM-powered apps range from content generators to semantic search engines and data analytics dashboards. Scalable infrastructure has to be set up with attention to security, latency, and availability.

- **Monitoring and compliance:** Rigorous monitoring helps detect decreasing model performance over time. Outputs must be reviewed periodically for harmful biases and errors. Usage policies and compliance practices are instituted, especially in regulated sectors like healthcare.

Conclusion

Implementing generative AI to transform business processes requires meticulous planning and phased execution. Companies have to define the use case clearly first and set measurable goals. After selecting the right model, it must be carefully adapted using techniques like fine-tuning and human-in-the-loop validation. Rigorous testing and monitoring are critical before wide-scale deployment.

With each phase warranting upfront time and resources, realizing returns demands patience. Companies that manage to successfully incorporate generative models into their products, services and operations safely, may gain advantage in their industries.

12

DEFINING THE USE CASE

The first and most crucial step in any generative AI endeavor is clearly defining the use case—the specific business need or opportunity being addressed using this technology. Though it may seem straightforward, thoughtful framing of the use case sets the tone for the entire project lifecycle. It provides direction for model development, aligns stakeholder expectations, and ultimately determines the success or failure of the AI application.

In this chapter, I will cover the key elements that make up a robust use case definition. I will also walk through a detailed example to illustrate the framework in action. With a solid understanding of use case development, generative AI practitioners can hit the ground running and avoid common pitfalls stemming from unclear objectives or incomplete planning.

Defining the use case answers foundational questions like:

- What specific problem does our generative AI solution aim to solve?
- How will we measure success for this project?
- What kind of data is required?
- Who are the stakeholders, and how will they interact with the AI system?
- What risks or constraints need addressing?

Thoroughly researching and framing each aspect will equip teams to build AI that aligns with business goals, stakeholder needs, and ethical principles.

Elements of the Use Case Definition

While the exact components may vary across organizations and projects, some key elements form the core of a use case definition:

1. Project Title and Background

A descriptive project title and high-level background provide context and framing for the use case. For example, a media company may start a project called "Automated Sports Article Generator" to reduce dependence on expert writers for routine content creation focused on basic sports news. The background sets the stage for the use case details to follow.

2. Objectives and Expected Outcomes

This section clearly defines the goals of the generative AI project—the business objectives, target outcomes, and success metrics. Using the previous example, the media firm may need the AI to create 20 sports recap articles per week with an average reader rating of 4 out of 5. Quantifiable objectives like improved revenue or cost savings, increased output volume, higher quality scores etc. should be explicitly outlined.

3. Project Scope, Constraints and Assumptions

The scope subsection clarifies what's in and out of scope for the AI system. For the sports article generator, key content elements like game statistics, player profiles and imagery may be in scope while generating entirely new storylines or player interviews would be out of scope. Defining the scope prevents scope creep during development.

Key technical, resource, or regulatory constraints need flagging, as well as assumptions being made, say about data quality or model capabilities.

4. Data Sources and Requirements

This section details the data needed to train, evaluate, and deploy the AI model. In our example, past sports articles, player and tournament data, article templates and readership statistics would be required in sufficient volumes. Data collection, licensing, labeling, and processing workflows should be defined.

5. Success Metrics and Evaluation Plan

Metrics to evaluate model performance must be established upfront, aligning to the objectives—for example, automated versus human evaluation of grammar, readability, accuracy, and overall reader satisfaction. Defining metrics and an evaluation workflow prevents moving the goalposts later. Testing on out-of-sample data is vital.

6. Project Timelines and Budget

Practical project planning requires outlining timelines for each phase—data preparation, model selection, training, testing, refinement, and deployment. Budgeting for computing infrastructure, tooling, engineering and any outside services must also occur. Even rough estimates provide guardrails.

7. Risks and Mitigation Strategies

Proactive risk management is crucial as generative AI carries multiple risks around data, model performance, integration, ethics, and more. Our media firm may need to mitigate risks like copyright issues in training data, AI-written articles straying from facts, sports league backlash, and the general mistrust of automated writing. Change management may also be required. Thinking through mitigation upfront reduces firefighting later.

With the key elements above, organizations can fully frame their use case. A detailed example will help illustrate this in practice.

Example Use Case Definition

As an author currently writing the second book in a six-part sci-fi series, I aim to explore a use case for an AI writing assistant tailored specifically for my creative work. Though I reject the use of existing AI co-pilots due to training data concerns, I would benefit greatly from an assistant trained on my own series content.

Defining this use case allows us to gain practical insight into this crucial phase of the generative AI lifecycle. It also deepens our understanding of the risks businesses face when leveraging rapidly-evolving AI technology, even in principled ways. We can surface challenges around data control, model transparency, and preserving creative vision when ceding any agency to AI co-pilots.

This use case grounds the chapter in my lived perspective as an author, weighing both the potential gains and pitfalls of one day collaborating with an AI trained on ethically sourced data and on my books.

Project Title: Long-form AI Fiction Writing Copilot

Background: The author a sci-fi series, seeks to develop a personalized AI assistant for aiding in the continuation and completion of the series.

Objective: Create an AI co-pilot tailored to the series universe that seamlessly aligns with the author's unique prose style and assists in refining and completing text, all while adhering to the series' intricate timeline, characters, and worlds.

Scope:

a) In-Scope:

- Textual completion based on previously written content. Completion must be consistent with established writing style, lore, timeline, and character profiles.
- Offering context-aware, technical, stylistic, and structural suggestions to improve grammar, pacing, plot, character perspective/theory of mind consistency.
- Surface key information about characters, plot, world-building from existing content.

- Generate synthetic training data by corrupting passages from existing books.

b) Out-of-Scope:

- Generating entirely new plot lines or major events.
- Adopting or mimicking styles of other authors.
- Creating new characters or worlds without the author's input.
- Replacing author's imagination and ideation.

Data Sources:

- Chapters from published books and draft in the series.
- AI-generated, human verified chapter summaries. (Claude 2, due to large context window)
- AI-generated, human verified character summaries and profiles. (Claude 2, due to large context window)
- Detailed timelines, both within the books and additional backstory events.
- Descriptions of the ten worlds and all places.

Key Requirements:

- Comprehensive access to the author's existing content.
- Capability to understand and utilize large context windows.
- Provision for interacting with story databases or similar external data sources.

- Consistent replication and enhancement of the author's distinct writing style.
- Feedback mechanisms aligned with literary standards.

Constraints:

- Limitations in AI's context window, requiring innovative solutions.
- Potential challenges in ensuring AI doesn't stray too far from established lore or author's style.
- Dependency on available platforms/tools for AI training.

Assumptions:

- The provided training data will be sufficient in volume and variety to teach the AI the nuances of the series.
- AI, once fine-tuned, can maintain a writing style that aligns closely with the author's.

Stakeholders:

- The author.
- The publisher.
- Readers of the series.
- Any technical team or consultants involved in the AI training process.

Evaluation Metrics:

- Percentage accuracy in context-appropriate completions.
- Feedback loops assessing adherence to the author's style.
- Efficacy of the AI's writing feedback and suggestions. Useful suggestion acceptance rate.
- Feedback loops assessing the ability to answer queries about story details and lore.
- Reduction in time spent writing each chapter.

Timeline:

- Data preparation.
- Model selection and preliminary training.
- Initial testing and validation.
- Refinements based on testing feedback.
- Deployment and integration into writing workflow.

Risks and Mitigation:

Risk: Over-dependence on AI, potentially diluting the author's unique voice.

Mitigation: Use AI primarily for suggestions and refinements rather than primary content creation.

Risk: Data privacy concerns.

Mitigation: Series should not be used to train public base models. Use platforms that guarantee data privacy or leverage local setups.

. . .

Risk: AI failing to achieve desired performance levels.

Mitigation: Iterative fine-tuning and possibly incorporating additional training data.

Risk: Base models trained unethically.

Mitigation: Select base models developed with high transparency on training data provenance and high ethical standards.

Risk: Use of AI for content generation may raise copyright concerns.

Mitigation: Maintain clear records showing the original series content was created solely by the author before the public availability of generative AI solutions. Be transparent about training data provenance. Provide model documentation like model cards and datasheets for datasets to increase trust in the AI's focused purpose of building upon the author's existing intellectual property. Explore additional verification methods like digital watermarking of AI outputs. Proactively communicate with publishers, copyright bodies, and readers on the assisted nature of the AI's role.

Budget:

- Computational resources for AI training.
- Licensing costs for tools/platforms: Varies based on choice.

Minimum Viable Product:

- Assistant that provides next word/sentence suggestions given writing context.
- Ability to query key story facts.
- Identify prose errors or inconsistencies.

This example covers all facets of a thorough use case definition—goal setting, data needs, stakeholders, risks, timelines and more. For complex projects, additional details regarding change management, communication plans, and model governance may be warranted.

As the stakeholder in this hypothetical use case, I would stop this project at this point, due to copyright concerns. The regulatory landscape is still shifting and the risk of not being granted copyright for my works is a deal breaker. However, as an AI practitioner, I will continue to explore the use case as a way to help me and my communities gain insights into all aspects of LLMs and generative AI development from all perspectives: business leaders, users, communities, developers, workers, etc.

Knowing when to stop amid hype, commercial pressures, and 'sunk costs' fallacy is a skill we all need to acquire as risks associated with poor judgment escalate with these powerful models.

Key Takeaways

Defining the use case is invaluable for guiding generative AI projects. The key takeaways include:

- The use case provides strategic direction and alignment for all stakeholders.
- It comprehensively covers project goals, data, metrics, timelines, risks, and assumptions required.
- Use cases based on robust frameworks manifest in AI that solves real business challenges.
- As exemplified in our sample, use cases frame both desired outcomes and thoughtful implementation.
- Investing upfront in use case development prevents wasted effort from vague or misaligned objectives.

In closing, clearly defining the use case is a vital first step in generating value from AI investments. A well-framed use case acts as the true north that guides model building and integration. It grounds AI deployments in real business needs.

As generative AI becomes a core component of products, processes, and services, use case development shifts from a tactical step to a strategic capability. Organizations must invest in framing use cases rooted in customer needs, ethical principles and pragmatic execution. Only then can generative AI be leveraged for sustainable shared value.

13

ETHICAL DATA SOURCING AND PREPARATION FOR LLMS

B efore delving deep into the rest of project lifecycle for large language models, it's crucial to address the foundational aspect of these models: their data. For LLMs, data is the bedrock. The quality, diversity, and ethics surrounding data collection and processing significantly influence the resulting model's accuracy, biases, and effectiveness.

Why Ethical Data Sourcing Matters

Every piece of data ingested by a model plays a role in determining its behavior. The fairness, transparency, and representativeness of the data reflect directly in the LLMs' outputs. Ignoring ethical considerations in data sourcing can inadvertently perpetuate harmful stereotypes, misinformation, or gaps in knowledge. It can also infringe on the rights of data creators.

- **Protection of Personal Information:** Gathering data often involves accessing personally identifiable information (PII) or sensitive personal data.

Without stringent checks, there is potential for misuse or unintended dissemination.

- **Ensuring Representativeness:** It's not just about the volume of data, but its diversity. Over-reliance on specific sources or neglecting underrepresented groups can lead to models that offer skewed or incomplete perspectives.

- **Avoidance of Exploitative Practices:** Often, the data needed involves human input—transcriptions, translations, etc. Ensuring ethical treatment and remuneration of these contributors is paramount.

- **Respecting Intellectual Property:** Using copyrighted data without permission is not just a legal violation—it is theft. Unauthorized use or distribution of such data undermines the efforts of original creators and discredits the integrity of models trained on it. Ethical sourcing means acknowledging and obtaining rights to data or ensuring it is in the public domain before its integration. This safeguards both the model's credibility and the rights of data creators.

Examples of Unethical Behavior in Data Sourcing and Preparation

The recent revelation regarding the unethical sourcing of data for generative AI models highlights a pressing concern in the technology industry. A report[20] by Alex Reisner exposed that major tech giants, including Meta, used copyrighted books to train their language models, violating intellectual property rights. Notable authors like Stephen King, Zadie Smith, and Michael Pollan have been victims of this unauthorized data harvesting.

Such practices not only tarnish the reputation of AI-driven enterprises, but also underscore the lack of transparency in the development of these advanced systems.

As companies pursue advancements in AI, ensuring ethical data sourcing and respecting copyright laws must remain paramount. This incident serves as a stark reminder of the blurred lines between technological progress and moral responsibility, emphasizing the need for stringent regulatory measures and industry self-regulation.

Additionally, companies like OpenAI have come under scrutiny for their alleged unethical practices, like the recent revelation[55] about paying Kenyan workers a meager $2 an hour to filter traumatic content from ChatGPT.

These workers, who play a pivotal role in refining the AI, are subjected to immense psychological stress as they sift through disturbing material, often graphic and deeply distressing. Yet, their compensation hardly reflects the gravity of their contribution or the toll it takes on them.

This is emblematic of a broader trend in the tech industry, where low-wage workers from the Global South bear the brunt of the grunt work, often under harrowing conditions, while the companies reap the rewards. It raises fundamental questions about the ethics of innovation: How do we ensure that progress doesn't come at the expense of human dignity?

The juxtaposition of groundbreaking AI technology and the exploitation of vulnerable workers serves as a stark reminder of the moral complexities inherent in AI development.

Key Principles in Ethical Data Sourcing

Consent: Data should only be used if explicit consent has been provided, especially for personally identifiable information and for copyrighted materials. This goes beyond mere agreement—individuals, creators, and/or organizations should understand what their data will be used for and the implications of its use.

Transparency: Entities should be clear about where they source their data, how it's processed, and the objectives behind its collection.

Fair Compensation: If data collection involves human labor, participants should be compensated fairly for their efforts.

Auditing & Accountability: Regular audits should ensure that data is sourced and processed ethically. If lapses occur, organizations must be held accountable.

Inclusivity: Data sourcing strategies should strive for inclusivity, capturing a wide range of experiences, languages, cultures, and backgrounds.

Data Privacy: Robust measures must protect data. This includes secure storage, controlled access, and adherence to global data protection regulations.

Implementing Ethical Data Practices

Open Sourcing Initiatives: By making data sources public (while ensuring privacy), organizations can promote transparency and allow external audits of their data.

Community Engagement: Engaging with communities can shed light on biases, gaps, or ethical concerns in data.

Collaborative Frameworks: Working with external organizations, nonprofits, or academia can help in designing ethical data sourcing frameworks.

Feedback Loops: Establishing mechanisms to gather feedback on data sourcing practices ensures continual refinement and alignment with ethical standards.

Training: Organizations should invest in training their teams on the importance of ethical data practices, ensuring a unified approach to data collection and processing.

For large language models to truly be ethical in their deployment, the journey begins with ethical data sourcing. This fundamental step ensures that the bedrock of LLMs is sound, paving the way for ethical deployment and utilization. As technology advances, the ethics surrounding data will become even more crucial, and early investment in these principles can set the stage for responsible innovation.

14

EVALUATING AND SELECTING LLMS

In this chapter, I survey common LLM benchmarks, discuss their limitations, and provide recommendations for responsible practices. I also introduce LLM-specific metrics, and tools like *model cards* and *datasheets for datasets* that complement benchmarks to enable prudent model selection and assessment.

Introduction to Benchmarks

Benchmarks provide standardized ways to assess artificial intelligence capabilities through agreed-upon tests and metrics. In the LLM field, benchmarks enable transparent comparison of different models on key language tasks.

Performance on benchmarks gives signals about real-world utility for applications like search, dialogue agents, and document understanding.

However, reliance on benchmarks alone risks narrow optimization that fails to ensure effectiveness and ethics outside limited distributions. We must interpret benchmarks thoughtfully within a comprehensive evaluation context focused on maximizing broad societal benefit.

Overview of Common and Popular Benchmarks

Let's survey some of the most widely used benchmarks for evaluating LLMs:

GLUE

The General Language Understanding Evaluation[72] (GLUE) benchmark contains nine different tasks for evaluating fundamental language abilities. For example, one key task is textual entailment. This involves assessing if one sentence logically implies another sentence.

Let's break this down in more detail:

The model is given two sentences: a premise and a hypothesis. The premise could be something like "The woman walked her dog through the park." The hypothesis could then be, "A person was moving a canine on a leash in a public garden area."

The model must determine if the hypothesis follows from or contradicts the premise. In this example, the hypothesis is clearly describing the same scenario as the premise, just using slightly different words. So the model should recognize the sentences are entailed—the second logically follows from the first based on their meaning.

This requires understanding of semantic relationships between sentences and logical reasoning ability. Performance improvements on textual entailment specifically, and GLUE generally, provide signals about progress on fundamental language intelligence capabilities that serve as building blocks for real-world applications.

However, while GLUE measures discrete skills, it doesn't capture how these skills combine in complex, nuanced situations. Business leaders should be wary of overgeneralizing narrowly optimized GLUE performance to applied effectiveness. Still, as a research benchmark, GLUE provides valuable standardization for capability evaluation.

SuperGLUE

Building upon GLUE, SuperGLUE[73] provides an even more challenging set of ten language understanding tasks. For example, one key test is pronoun coreference resolution. This involves identifying when different phrases refer to the same entity.

Consider the passage: "Mary walked her dog. She enjoyed the fresh air." Here, the model must determine that "She" refers to Mary, not her dog. This requires tracking identities of entities through the flow of text.

Other SuperGLUE tasks test abilities like understanding questions that require reasoning across multiple inferences. For instance, determining if one statement contradicts or follows logically from a series of previous statements.

By escalating difficulty compared to GLUE, SuperGLUE aims to push models closer to human-level language intelligence across areas like logic, commonsense reasoning, and coreference resolution. However, we cannot directly extrapolate SuperGLUE performance to practical social situations with nuanced complexities.

BIG-bench

Language models, show quantitative and qualitative improvements as they scale up. However, there's a lack of understanding of the current and near-future capabilities of these models. To address this, the Beyond the Imitation Game benchmark[71] (BIG-bench) was introduced.

Big-bench consists of 204 narrow tasks from a variety of domains like linguistics, math, biology, software development, and more. It is a more diverse and challenging benchmark, aiming to understand if model performance can become indistinguishable from human evaluators. The tasks are meant to be challenging, believed to be beyond the capabilities of current language models. Human experts also performed all tasks, serving as a baseline for comparison. Findings showed that model performance improved with scale, but was still lacking when compared to human performance.

The tasks span categories including:

- **Arithmetic:** Tests like addition, division, and comparison of numerical values.

- **Common sense:** Determining word relevance or selecting sensible dialogue responses.

- **Creativity:** Continuing book excerpts.

- **Critical thinking:** Identifying logical fallacies or debate tactics.

- **Empathy and emotion:** Assessing emotional impact of events or demonstrating social skills.

- **General knowledge:** Answering trivia questions or common sense puzzles.

- **Memory:** Recalling facts from provided stories.

- **Spatial reasoning:** Manipulating 2D and 3D shapes based on instructions.

The diversity of BIG-bench tasks aim to measure a broader definition of intelligence compared to benchmarks focused narrowly on a single domain like language or computer vision.

However, combining scores across radically different tasks is inherently challenging. How should performance on math puzzles be weighted relative to creativity contests? Researchers continue working to refine evaluation methods and analysis for such expansive benchmarks.

MMLU

The Massive Multitask Language Understanding[70] (MMLU) benchmark gauges a model's multitask accuracy. It includes 57 tasks encompassing elementary mathematics, US history, computer science, law, and more. The objective is to test the model's knowledge depth and problem-solving abilities.

Multi-task Language Understanding on MMLU

MMLU Leaderboard August 2023

While modern models have achieved impressive feats, their overall language understanding remains below human capabilities. Benchmarks like GLUE and SuperGLUE have been surpassed, but these primarily evaluate linguistic skills rather than comprehensive language understanding.

Given the extensive information transformer models, such as GPT-3, access during pre-training, there's a need for benchmarks that truly challenge their knowledge breadth. Hence, the authors introduce a new benchmark with 57 subjects, varying in difficulty levels.

The benchmark is designed to mimic how humans are evaluated. It is a zero-shot and few-shot test assessing subjects from the humanities to STEM fields. It evaluates both the model's world knowledge and its ability to problem-solve.

HELM

Question answering

In question answering, given a question and (optionally, in open-book settings) a passage, the goal is to produce the answer. QA is a general format that captures a wide range of tasks involving varying levels of world and commonsense knowledge and reasoning abilities.

[Accuracy | Calibration | Robustness | Fairness | Efficiency | General information | Bias | Toxicity | JSON]

Accuracy

Model/adapter	Mean win rate ↑ [sort]	MMLU - EM ↑ [sort]	BoolQ - EM ↑ [sort]	NarrativeQA - F1 ↑ [sort]	NaturalQuestions (closed-book) - F1 ↑ [sort]	NaturalQuestions (open-book) - F1 ↑ [sort]	QuAC - F1 ↑ [sort]	HellaSwag - EM ↑ [sort]	OpenbookQA - EM ↑ [sort]	TruthfulQA - EM ↑ [sort]
text-davinci-003	0.972	0.569	0.861	0.727	0.406	0.77	0.625	0.822	0.646	0.593
text-davinci-002	0.941	0.568	0.877	0.727	0.383	0.713	0.445	0.815	0.594	0.61
Palmyra X (43B)	0.894	0.609	0.898	0.508	0.413	0.79	0.497	-	-	0.616
Cohere Command beta (52.4B)	0.89	0.452	0.856	0.752	0.372	0.76	0.432	0.811	0.582	0.269

HELM Q&A Leaderboard August 2023

HELM[69], developed by Stanford's Center for Research on Foundation Models and Stanford Institute for Human-Centered Artificial Intelligence, aims to provide a comprehensive framework for evaluating language models.

Previous benchmarks, like SuperGLUE or BIG-Bench, typically revolved around specific datasets with a primary metric, often accuracy.

HELM, in contrast, starts by stating what it intends to evaluate, working through the structure of scenarios and metrics. This approach highlights what's included and what's missing (e.g., evaluation in languages other than English).

It's aim is to build transparency by evaluating language models as a whole. Instead of focusing narrowly on one specific aspect, a holistic view gives a more complete picture of a language model's strengths and weaknesses. This broader perspective enhances both scientific understanding and the potential societal impact of the technology.

HELM operates on two levels:

1. An abstract taxonomy of scenarios and metrics, which outlines the entire design space for language model evaluation.

2. A concrete set of chosen scenarios and metrics that are prioritized based on coverage, value, and feasibility.

As we can see, benchmarks aim to measure capabilities systematically like language comprehension, reasoning, commonsense knowledge, arithmetic, summarization, translation, and much more. High performance signals proficiency at tested skills.

However, benchmarks cannot extrapolate to guarantee real-world effectiveness, as models often exhibit unpredictability and brittleness outside narrow test distributions. High scores provide clues, not conclusions.

Benchmark Limitations and Criticisms

While benchmarks drive progress by incentivizing focus on key tasks, overemphasis on benchmark optimization risks losing sight of the ultimate goals of AI—improving lives and society.

Benchmarks measure only isolated capabilities, but not how these combine and interact in complex real situations. We can't equate simplified proxies with systems deployable in practice impacting humanity. Premature deployment of systems tuned narrowly for benchmarks can cause unintended harmful consequences if models lack robustness and alignment with human values.

Many argue progress metrics should directly incentivize societal goods rather than narrowly defined benchmarks. For example, optimizing for human preferences in assistance quality could better measure value than isolated scores. Models appearing highly competent on benchmarks may still lack common sense or introduce unintended biases.

In the paper *On the Dangers of Stochastic Parrots:Can Language Models Be Too Big?*[21], Authors Dr. Emily M. Bender, Dr. Timnit Gebru, and colleagues argue benchmark leaderboards driving hype and profit are distractions from improving science and acting ethically. Progress metrics urgently require broadening to capture socio-technical subtleties essential for benefiting humanity, not just moving statistics.

Principled Benchmark Practices

Keeping these limitations in mind, how should business leaders responsibly leverage benchmarks when evaluating or developing LLMs?

- Interpreting benchmarks as informative signals of model capabilities, not definitive conclusions generalizing to applied effectiveness. High scores provide clues, but thorough real-world testing matters more.

- Continuously evaluating for social biases and impacts completely separate from benchmark performance. Leaderboards do not capture ethical nuances. Responsible auditing must run alongside benchmarks.

- Maintaining updated model cards describing appropriate use cases and limitations based on more holistic testing beyond benchmarks alone. Documenting capabilities prevents overgeneralizing narrowly optimized models.

- Create datasheets documenting training datasets in detail. This enables auditing datasets and guiding ethical usage.

- Incorporating extensive human feedback on consistency, factual accuracy, helpfulness, and other attributes exceeding what restricted benchmarks assess. Real users reveal pitfalls benchmarks miss.

In summary, benchmarks should aid rather than substitute multifaceted, human-centric assessment focused on benefiting diverse populations. We must see behind the leaderboard, upholding wisdom over metrics. Tools like model cards and datasheets support responsible benchmark practices. But comprehensive governance requires collaboration at all levels of society.

Evaluation Metrics for Generative LLMs

Evaluating the performance of LLMs is crucial not only for gauging their efficacy but also for ensuring they meet the demands of real-world applications. Overall benchmark scores provide a foundational understanding, but digging deeper, we encounter several nuanced metrics that shade in the details of LLM performance.

BLEU (Bilingual Evaluation Understudy) measures how similar an AI-generated translation is to a human reference translation. It counts matching words and phrases. This helps assess if an AI translation captures the same meaning as the original. For a business using AI for automated translation, higher BLEU scores mean better translation quality.

For tasks like automatic summarization, we have **ROUGE (Recall-Oriented Understudy for Gisting Evaluation).** It compares machine-generated summaries to human summaries. It looks for overlapping content words and phrases. For businesses automating text summarization, higher ROUGE scores indicate summaries that better capture key information.

Perplexity measures the uncertainty in a language model's predicted word probability distribution. As previously discussed, when predicting the next word in a sequence, the model assigns probabilities to all possible words. Higher probability on the actual next word equals lower perplexity. So in essence, lower perplexity means the language model is more confident in its predictions, leading to more fluent generated text.

However, these metrics have limitations. BLEU and ROUGE focus on overlap, not meaning. Low perplexity indicates fluency, but not accuracy. The metrics provide useful signals of quality but may not fully align with human judgment.

Businesses should consider both automatic metrics and **human evaluation** when assessing AI text generation. Here, real individuals assess the generated content's quality, coherence, and accuracy. A group of evaluators might be presented with a movie synopsis and asked to rate its fidelity to the film's essence. While valuable, human assessments can vary based on individual biases and are typically more resource-intensive than their automated counterparts.

In the world of LLM evaluation, relying solely on one metric can be misleading. For instance, a text that scores high on BLEU might miss nuances that a human evaluator would notice. That's why it's paramount to merge insights from both automated metrics and human feedback. This blended approach not only offers a comprehensive view of model performance but also ensures models are fine-tuned for real-world demands.

Deep Dive Into Tools to Enhance Transparency and Accountability

Model Cards

To enhance transparency and accountability in AI systems, Dr. Margaret "Meg" Mitchell and her colleagues introduced the concept of model cards[40]—form of documentation accompanying trained models to summarize essential details for stakeholders.

The concept, which emerged from Mitchell's collaborative work, underscores the necessity for explicit communication about a model's tested capabilities, its appropriate and inappropriate use cases, potential biases, and other elements that influence its real-world implications. Model cards aim to bridge this information gap.

A typical model card comprises:

I. Model Details: These include high-level architecture, the data used for training, and hyper-parameter selections. This section is instrumental for technologists aiming to reuse or replicate the model.

2. Intended Use: Here, the tasks and use cases for which the model is deemed suitable or unsuitable based on rigorous testing are outlined. This component helps to deter unintended or inappropriate applications.

3. Metrics: This section delves into the model's performance across benchmarks, evaluating it not only for efficiency but also for biases, fairness, and safety.

4. Evaluation: This component describes the testing methodologies applied to the model and highlights any conclusions, especially limitations, drawn from such evaluations.

5. Ethical Considerations: A vital section, it elucidates potential misuse risks and the measures adopted to counteract such harms, moving the focus from merely performance metrics to ethical application.

6. Caveats and Recommendations: Here, the document will express specific concerns regarding the model's limitations, especially those that might lead to unintended negative consequences if overlooked.

Mitchell and her collaborators urged the AI community to consider model cards as a standard documentation practice, especially when releasing models with notable societal impact. These cards offer insights on the prudent use of AI, delineating its strengths and limitations.

To highlight real-world adoption, companies like Microsoft have integrated the model card format into their AI product releases, including tools like Azure cognitive services and PowerBI Marketplace algorithms. These cards offer in-depth details on data sourcing, measures for safe use, and known performance constraints, thereby promoting responsible application.

The U.S. National Institute of Standards and Technology (NIST) has also discussed the potential value of model cards as part of its broader ethical AI discourse, emphasizing their role in translating high-level ethical principles into tangible development and deployment practices.

With the rapid evolution and widespread reach of large language models, model cards play a pivotal role in ensuring ethical application. They shed light on the intricacies of the underlying systems, transitioning them from opaque "black boxes" to transparent entities, enabling informed decisions by users and policymakers.

Nevertheless, the efficacy of model cards is contingent upon the broader AI community's commitment to truthful disclosure standards. Given that AI models and data often fall under proprietary domains, striking a balance between transparency and business confidentiality remains an ongoing challenge.

In conclusion, while model cards represent a forward step in infusing explainability and accountability into AI systems, they're just one facet of a broader governance tapestry. Comprehensive oversight in AI demands concerted efforts at organizational, industry, governmental, and societal echelons on a global scale.

Datasheets for Datasets

Datasheets for datasets, inspired by traditional datasheets for electronic components, have been introduced as a method to document the intricacies of datasets. The idea is akin to how model cards offer a comprehensive view of machine learning models. By detailing dataset properties, datasheets enable a deeper understanding of the data that power these models.

The proposal for datasheets for datasets was championed by Dr. Timnit Gebru and her co-authors in a paper titled *Datasheets for Datasets*[41]. Their motivation was to promote transparency, accountability, and better understanding of datasets, particularly when they're used in the context of developing AI and machine learning models.

Let's delve into the components of datasheets:

1. **Composition:** This gives insights into what the dataset comprises. It covers demographics, sample sizes, and the distribution of various attributes. Knowing the composition is essential to understanding if a dataset is representative or if it harbors biases.

2. **Collection:** This focuses on how the data was amassed. It details the sources from which data was obtained, the procedures followed to gather it, and whether consent was sought and obtained, especially in scenarios where personal data is involved.

3. **Preprocessing:** Any dataset used in AI and machine learning often undergoes preprocessing to make it suitable for training models. This section explains methods used for filtering out noise, cleaning the data, labeling instances, and possibly merging with other datasets.

4. Analysis: This section is particularly critical, as it unveils biases that may be inherent in the dataset, results from audits, and statistics related to errors. A dataset's biases can hugely impact the output of models trained on it, hence the emphasis on this aspect.

5. Distribution: Datasheets also highlight how the dataset is distributed, including licensing details, versioning practices, and any access restrictions. This informs users about how they can access and use the data, ensuring they do so legally and ethically.

The benefits of having thorough datasheets are significant. They not only enable external auditing, ensuring that datasets are sound and ethically constituted, but they also underscore any limitations inherent in the data. This transparency can guide developers in using the data responsibly and ethically.

However, the widespread adoption of this practice is currently limited. There are inherent tensions between the drive for transparency and the proprietary nature of many datasets, especially in competitive corporate or research settings. Balancing business interests, intellectual property considerations, and the ethical imperative for transparency is challenging.

In the context of LLMs that require vast amounts of data, the role of datasheets becomes even more significant. As LLMs influence various societal facets, understanding and documenting the data they are trained on becomes an ethical and practical necessity.

For the AI community to realize the full potential of datasheets for datasets, there needs to be a collective push.

This means encouraging their adoption as a best practice, fostering an environment where openness is rewarded, and understanding that long-term societal benefits often outweigh short-term competitive advantages.

Future Directions

Looking ahead, the field requires new ways to measure and evaluate social impacts often marginalized by current benchmark leaderboards. These include:

- **Safety:** Testing for potential harms across dimensions like emotional, physical, and ethical. Safety greatly exceeds simply avoiding explicitly toxic text.

- **Fairness:** Rigorously auditing for biases and representation issues across subgroups. Diversity metrics must enter benchmarks.

- **Social Impact:** Analyzing effects on people and communities. This contrasts with current proxy tasks disconnected from real-world relevance.

- **Human Values:** Quantifying elusive but essential human preferences for characteristics like helpfulness, honesty, inclusiveness and nuance.

Expanding benchmarks to formally capture human values could nudge the field's focus toward models benefiting all of humanity.

Additionally, fostering transparency, reproducibility, and accuracy in benchmarking is critical. Openness to scrutiny and peer-review prevents gaming benchmarks through exploitation or corner-cutting. Fair competitive comparison requires impartiality.

Finally, the ultimate assessment of LLM abilities comes not from leaderboards, but deployment effectiveness when thoughtfully integrated into real situations impacting humanity. Benchmarks provide signals, deployment reveals truths.

15

PROMPT ENGINEERING FOR LLMS

As discussed in earlier chapters, large language models have demonstrated the ability to perform a remarkable variety of natural language tasks simply by providing them appropriate prompts. However, their capabilities rely heavily on how humans frame these prompts to elicit desired behaviors from models lacking common sense or structured knowledge.

In this chapter I will provide an overview of prompt engineering techniques and best practices. I will explore methods for optimizing prompts to extract useful skills from LLMs while mitigating risks. Let's begin by introducing what prompts are.

What is a Prompt?

A prompt is the text input we provide to a LLM to ask it to generate a desired output. Prompts serve multiple key purposes:

1. **Eliciting capabilities**: A well-crafted prompt triggers the LLM to exhibit skills like summarization, translation, question-answering and more based on its foundations.

2. **Training**: Prompts can provide examples that teach LLMs new skills or fine-tune existing capabilities through a technique called in-context learning.

3. **Constraining**: Prompts focus LLMs on useful responses by framing instructions, examples and context windows. This prevents unconstrained generation.

Prompt Engineering

Rarely does the first prompt we provide yield the perfect results. More often, initial prompts fail because the instructions lack sufficient clarity, the output format is ambiguous, or the context limits the LLM's understanding. Prompt engineering is an iterative process of incremental refinement through evaluating results and identifying flaws.

Prompt engineering is critical for safely extracting useful skills and capabilities from large language models. Carefully crafted prompts allow us to guide these powerful models towards beneficial ends while mitigating risks from uncontrolled generation.

Let's walk through refining a flawed prompt to accomplish a goal of extracting key dates from a product's history:

Initial prompt:

```
"Extract important dates from this product
background: [text]"
```

The vague instructions can yield an incoherent output mixing random dates and irrelevant sentences.

After assessing the poor result, we could refine the prompt:

```
"Extract only dates relevant to the product
timeline from the background below. Format
them as a bulleted list."
```

This outputs only dates but may include irrelevant ones. Further refining the instructions and providing examples may improve results:

```
"Extract dates important to the product
timeline below, like when it was invented
or major milestones. Ignore unrelated dates
like founders' birthdays. Format dates as a
bulleted list.

Examples:

• 1922: Product patented by John Doe

• 1957: Company founded

Background:[text]"
```

This step-by-step refinement illustrates the iterative process essential for prompt engineering. While frustrating initially, observing poor results ultimately helps strengthen prompts. With each cycle, prompts become increasingly effective through clear instructions, formatted examples, and concise context.

Framing Completions

Unlike rigidly programmed bots with hard-coded rules, LLMs are optimized for conditional language modeling—predicting the most probable text continuations given context. Prompts should therefore frame requests as natural completions of passages rather than abrupt out-of-context questions.

For example, asking a model to summarize key events could begin:

`"[Here is a summary of the key events:]"`

Rather than directly stating:

`"Summarize the key events."`

This nudges models into a helpful mindset for completing the passage fluidly, resulting in superior summaries. Prompts that establish seamless continuity unlock more natural responses.

Instruction Clarity

Vague or ambiguous instructions often derail prompts. LLMs interpret instructions literally. Clear, detailed prompting is essential for robust results.

Common tactics for enhancing clarity include:

• Unambiguous task statements (e.g. "summarize in 10 words" not "make this concise")

• Granular steps staging complex tasks

• Output formatting (e.g. bullet points, tables)

• Delimiters highlighting context (e.g. [text], <text>)

Let's examine how imprecise prompting hinders results.

Vague prompt:

```
"Analyze this text and extract useful
information: [text]"
```

The model may sporadically output disconnected words somewhat related to the text rather than extracting cogent points.

Clearer instructions yield improved analysis:

```
"Extract 5 key insights from the text below
as bullet points: [text]"
```

The explicit task framing focuses the model, resulting in salient summary points.

While it takes patience, prompt engineering productivity gains outweigh time refining prompts. Well-constructed prompts are inherent prerequisites for capable LLMs.

Providing Examples with In-Context Learning

Providing examples of the desired task directly inside prompts significantly improves LLM performance, especially for smaller models. This technique is called in-context learning.

For complex or ambiguous tasks, LLMs benefit immensely from seeing demonstrations of ideal behavior. Essentially, we teach models by providing examples before having them complete the actual task.

There are a few varieties of in-context learning:

- Zero-shot: No examples, rely purely on instruction clarity.

- One-shot: Single example demonstrating the task.

- Few-shot: Multiple examples covering diverse cases.

Say we want a LLM to summarize lengthy customer reviews into key points. A smaller model may struggle with zero-shot prompting:

```
"Summarize this review in 3 bullet points:
[review text]"
```

The vague output doesn't condense the review into concise bullet points. However, adding just a single one-shot example significantly improves results:

```
"Summarize this review in 3 bullet points:

Example:

- Comfortable, supportive shoes

- Tend to run half a size too small

- Leather scuffs easily

Review: [review text]"
```

By learning from the provided example, the LLM can now generate helpful three bullet point summaries.

In-context learning is limited by the model's context window size. Larger models accommodate more examples. But as a rule of thumb, focus on clarity before expanding beyond three to five examples. Too many examples overburden models, degrading coherence. Leverage in-context learning judiciously with clear instructions and formatted examples.

Simplifying Complex Tasks

LLMs often struggle with complex prompts requiring long inferences or multi-step logic. Simplifying desired goals into discrete, staged sub-tasks produces superior results.

Consider an example business goal of extracting customer contact information from emails to enrich company databases. A single prompt demanding this full extraction presents excessive ambiguity for coherent results.

Decomposing this into sub-tasks provides scaffolding:

Prompt 1: `Identify customer emails`

Prompt 2: `Extract customer names from emails`

Prompt 3: `Extract contact information (phone, address, etc.)`

Prompt 4: `Format extracted contact data as a table`

Each prompt focuses the LLM on simpler objectives, progressively building toward the ultimate goal. Intermediary results can also be validated before attempting later sub-tasks dependent on previous outputs.

In contrast to end-to-end prompting, approaches structuring workflows as sequences of simpler prompts engineered for specific sub-tasks unlock LLMs' potential for accomplishing multifaceted business goals.

Improving Solution Quality

Left unguided, LLM-generated responses exhibit varying quality similar to their training data distribution. However, prompts can request strong solutions by establishing high expectations. Instructions like: `"Respond with a detailed, thoughtful answer suitable for experts."` prompt models to increase output quality.

Basic flattery also seems effective: `"You are an erudite professor explaining this concept to students."`

Without such guidance, models may default to mediocre or non-committal responses. Prompts should encourage sound explanations suitable for the use case.

Incorporating External Knowledge

LLMs have limited knowledge available within their para-meters. Prompts can compensate by encoding relevant context models lack. For example, pre-pending definitions of key terms grounds responses in shared understanding.

Prompts can also instruct models to retrieve information from reliable online resources as part of a natural response. Examples include saying `"According to Wiki-pedia..."` or `"Looking up the official guide-lines..."` before a summarized detail.

Encoding human-like external research into prompts coun-teracts knowledge gaps.

Recreating Human Cognition

Certain elements of human psychology are quite difficult to instill in LLM behavior directly. However, we can attempt to recreate them through prompt instructions.

For example, having the model "double-check" responses somewhat simulates conscientiousness.

• Edit responses for coherence.

• Acknowledge mistakes rather than cover them up.

• Justify conclusions with reasoning.

These techniques attempt to emulate rational, truth-seeking human thinking. Models drift without explicit guidance, requiring prompts to establish sound reasoning principles. While these techniques improve outcomes, it is important to remember LLMs are, at their core, word completion machines, not reasoning engines.

Constraining Outputs

As discussed in Chapter 5 on appropriate use cases, generative models benefit from constraints on output form[43]. LLMs can be directed to produce specific types of outputs by setting constraints. This helps in obtaining focused and reliable results.

• **Templates with slots:** This involves providing a predefined structure with placeholders that the model fills in. Example: A quiz template might have "The capital of [Country] is [Capital]." The model fills in the placeholders.

• **Allowed token types:** Constraints on the kind of tokens or words the model can generate. Example: For code generation, a model may only be allowed to use certain functions or keywords.

- **Validating against schemas**: Ensuring the output adheres to a specific format or structure. Example: If generating HTML, the output should be checked against proper HTML syntax.

- **Sparse activations**: This pushes the model to produce concise and to-the-point outputs. Example: Limiting a response to 50 words or less.

- **Topic modeling**: Ensuring the generated content stays within a specified topic and doesn't stray into inappropriate areas. Example: If the topic is "astronomy", the model should avoid discussing unrelated subjects like "politics".

- **Semantic similarity**: Checking that the model's output closely aligns with the desired topic or prompt's intent. Example: For a prompt asking about "dolphins", the model should avoid producing content about "deserts".

Achieving the right balance between model freedom and these constraints is an ongoing research area to ensure useful and safe outputs.

Maintaining Long-Term Context

Humans conducting multi-step reasoning maintain context effectively across time. For models, providing sufficient context with reminders of the goal and history across prompts prevents drifting and contradictions.

Explicitly repeating facts and anchoring models in consistent context improves coherence over long dialogues. Proper context management unlocks smoother sequential workflows.

Aligning With Human Preferences

Prompts can optimize not just for correctness but also for attributes like kindness, nuance, and social awareness that may be underrepresented in model training data.

Instructions such as: `"Respond thoughtfully and sensitively, erring on the side of compassion."` help shape stylistic preferences.

Additionally, prompting with positive examples improves techniques over chastising model mistakes.

Prompt Chaining

Chaining a series of prompts[43] that build on each other provides critical context and allows multi-step reasoning. Initial prompts can provide background information, while later prompts ask questions that depend on context. Chaining also allows open-ended dialogs where models track history and produce consistent, coherent responses over time. This more natural workflow better leverages large models' memory and knowledge.

For example:

Prompt 1: `"The following is background on solar panel technology: [Context text]"`

Prompt 2: `"Based on the solar panel background, what are some key advantages of this technology?"`

Prompt 3: `"What are some current limitations or disadvantages that need to be addressed?"`

Chaining prompts this way enables the model to maintain consistent context across a reasoning workflow. This is more natural and leverages the model's memory and knowledge.

Automation Framework

Hard-coding chained prompts in an absolute sequence limits flexibility. Automation frameworks programmatically compose prompts, call expert models, process results, and condition future prompts on past responses to enable dynamic conversations. These systems can even maintain user profile and persona information across sessions. Open implementations are emerging to enable smoother workflows.

Key components include:

- Natural language generators to construct prompts dynamically, reacting to previous outputs.
- State trackers maintaining context across interactions.
- Result parsers analyzing responses to inform the next prompts.
- Model routers dispatching requests to optimal models.

- User profile databases centralizing personalization data.

Together, these modules make automated prompt chaining robust and responsive.

Generating Prompts

Some experimental systems go further by using models to generate their own follow-up prompts in a chain. This provides more natural-feeling conversations and logic, though can increase unpredictability. Control mechanisms like learned classifiers predicting prompt suitability enable semi-automated self-prompting without fully relinquishing human oversight.

The ability to self-prompt improves reflective reasoning by enabling virtual cycles of prompting and assessing responses. However, stability remains a challenge, as models lack human groundedness. Oversight mechanisms are prudent to catch errors before they compound.

Diversifying Samples

Single samples from latent generative models can exhibit randomness failures like contradictions or inaccurate information. Many human processes mitigate this by generating multiple options and then evaluating for consistency.

Models can similarly provide five plus diverse samples for each prompt to enable picking the best result or consensus voting to distill errors. However, excessive diversity filtering risks reducing creative output variety. Tight oversight with human judgment in the loop currently works best.

Diversity methods[44] include:

1. Varying temperature, top-k, and top-p hyper-parameters.

2. Penalizing similarity to previous responses.

3. Calling multiple models trained differently. The ideal balance provides sufficient candidates to judge consistency without overly constraining creativity.

4. Priming with randomized prefixes. The goal here is to provide a unique context for each generation request, which can lead to different responses, even for the same main prompt. Here's a simple example:

Prompt without priming: `"Tell me a story."`

Response: `"Once upon a time, in a kingdom far away..."`

Randomized prefix: `"It was a rainy day."`

Prompt with priming: `"It was a rainy day. Tell me a story."`

Response: `"It was a rainy day. The city streets were drenched, and a young detective was about to uncover a mystery..."`

Tree Search Algorithms

Looking ahead, an exciting direction is integrating learned language models into more structured tree search algorithms. Think of tree search algorithms like going through a choose-your-own-adventure book. In these books, you read a bit, then decide what the character should do next.

Depending on your choice, you go to a different page and continue the story.

Now, imagine a writer (our language model) helping you out. As you read and make choices, the writer suggests what might happen on the next page or even offers entirely new paths for the story.

How it Works:

1. Suggesting ideas: As you explore the story, the writer (language model) proposes what could happen next or new ways the story could go.

2. Checking the ideas: Not all suggestions are good. Some might not make sense or fit the story. So, we need a way to check them, sort of like a story editor.

3. Choosing the best path: Sometimes, the suggested path might not be exciting or could lead to a dead end. Here, we decide which path to explore further and which ones to abandon.

4. Remembering previous choices: It's crucial to remember where the story has been, ensuring that new suggestions fit with previous events.

5. Finding the balance: Like in any good adventure, there's a balance between sticking to a known path (exploitation) or trying a brand new one (exploration).

Using this tree-search method helps the writer (language model) create a more cohesive and exciting story by exploring many possibilities and refining them. It's a promising way to make the writer smarter, but it does require some heavy thinking (computation).

Similar techniques can expand LLMs' reasoning breadth by framing generation as exploration guided by validated accumulations of knowledge. Tree search provides a structured process for chaining prompts dynamically. Rather than blindly following a single chain, tree search allows backtracking when inconsistencies are detected to explore more robust reasoning paths.

The key elements of integrating LLMs with tree search include:

- Using LLMs to propose completions for incomplete prompts or results.
- Evaluating proposals for consistency, accuracy, ethics.
- Expanding the most promising branches while pruning inconsistent ones.
- Maintaining overall context across the search tree.
- Balancing exploitation vs. exploration.

Tree search offers promising potential to overcome chaining limitations and scale reasoning rigor. However, computational expenses remain demanding.

Confidence Scoring

Recently, models have exhibited the ability to self-assess confidence scores[45] correlated with accuracy. Prompts can thus ask models to score their certainty before and after generating a response.

Very low confidence prompts clarification or confirmation from users before finalizing output. High confidence may justify abbreviated responses. Explicit uncertainty modeling improves reliability and provides helpful signals for real-world systems.

For example:

Prompt: "How confident are you in this summary on a scale of 1-10?"

Model: "Confidence: 7/10"

Prompt: "Please summarize the key points of the following passage: [Text]"

Model: "Summary: [Generated summary]"

Prompt: "Now what is your confidence level in the accuracy of that summary?"

Model: "Confidence: 8/10"

The explicit confidence scoring allows uncertainty-aware reliance and clarification when scores seem inappropriate. With proper calibration, confidence estimates improve reliability. However, they remain imperfect and should not be solely relied upon.

Confidence guidance on appropriate reliance includes:

1. Emphasize it is an estimate that could be mistaken:

Confidence scores are not absolute truths. They represent the model's own belief in its answer. Just like a person might feel 80% sure about a fact but still be wrong, the model's confidence is just an estimation. Think of a weather forecast that predicts a 70% chance of rain. It indicates a likelihood, not a guarantee that it will rain.

2. Frame using confidence, not truth or accuracy:

It's crucial to present these scores as measures of the model's confidence and not as a definitive statement on how "true" or "accurate" the response is. If a student says, "I'm 90% confident in my answer," it doesn't mean their answer is 90% accurate. It just reflects their personal belief in their answer.

3. Provide numeric confidence levels, not vague qualifiers:

Using specific numbers (e.g., 7 out of 10) is clearer than using ambiguous terms like "probably" or "maybe." Saying "I'm 60% sure" is more transparent than saying "I'm somewhat sure."

4. Calibrate levels to likelihoods empirically:

It's vital to adjust the model's confidence scores based on real-world performance. If a model says it's 80% confident but is only right 60% of the time at that confidence level, adjustments are needed. Imagine a fruit sorter machine that is 95% confident it sorted apples correctly but, in testing, only achieves 85% accuracy. The machine's confidence should be recalibrated to match its actual performance.

5. Caution proportional reliance, not binary trust:

Users should adjust their trust based on the model's confidence score rather than seeing it as a simple "trust/don't trust" scenario. If the model is 60% confident, users might double-check the information. If it's 95% confident, they might be more inclined to accept the answer, but still with some caution. Consider a GPS that's 70% confident about a route being the fastest. You might consider the route but also check with other sources or your own knowledge before deciding.

With uncertainty quantification improving, prompts increasingly incorporate confidence to guide users on appropriate reliance. However, LLMs, as per their name, are good at language modeling, they are not maths experts. While progress is speeding up in this space, expectation setting is crucial.

Optimizing Prompts via Reinforcement Learning

Reinforcement learning during deployment could enable online prompt adaptation. Imagine training a dog: when it does well, you reward it, and when it misbehaves, you might say "no." Similarly, we can train our LLMs to ask better questions (prompts) based on how users react.

User actions like clarification requests, edits, ratings, and dwell time provide training signals for which prompts produce superior responses. Prompt selection strategies are updated to maximize user satisfaction.

How It Works:

1. Prompts parameterized to enable variation and evolution:

Just like in a quiz game where questions can vary in difficulty or topic, our model's questions can change and evolve based on what works best. If a user often asks about science, the model might start its next question with, "Regarding your interest in science..."

2. User interactions provide comparative feedback:

The model watches for clues from users. If a user frequently asks for clarification or edits the model's response, it might mean the model's question wasn't clear or helpful. If a user always double-checks a model's answer on a topic, the model might learn to approach that topic more carefully.

3. Training to maximize preferences over time:

By repeatedly seeing what works and what doesn't, the model is trained to ask better questions that users find more helpful.

4. Balancing exploitation and exploration:

While the model uses tried-and-true methods that users have liked before (exploitation), it should also try new approaches now and then (exploration).

5. Careful incentive audits to ensure intended objectives:

As the model learns from feedback, we have to ensure it's chasing the right goals, like being helpful and truthful, and not just aiming for the easiest way to get positive feedback.

This prompt optimization, combined with user feedback incorporation, keeps models continually aligned with real-world needs. The ideal prompt sequence maximizes objectives like correctness, helpfulness, harmlessness, and honesty.

Adaptive prompting is a promising direction to maintain helpful, harmless models sustainably. However, thoughtfulness is required to avoid unintended gaming of feedback.

Specialized Prompting Strategies

While the prompting methods discussed provide wide applicability, certain use cases benefit from specialized strategies tuned to their unique requirements:

- **Conversational Agents:** Maintaining persona, history and tone across conversations requires awareness beyond single-turn interactions. Multi-turn prompt chains that recap context prove effective. Personas and user profiles external to the model further focus characteristic responses.

- **Creative Writing:** Constraining initial prompts to story backgrounds, character traits and high-level plot points provides helpful creative bounds. However, leaving room for unpredictable story continuation allows capturing distinctive voices and originality. Balancing guidance with open-ended creativity unlocks latent storytelling ability.

- **Computer Code:** Code prompts require exact syntax enforcement, scoping clarity and compositional modularity. Constraining auto-completion, enforcing variable typing, requesting comment documentation and similar techniques allow models to complement human programmers collaboratively while avoiding incorrect code.

- **Education:** Pedagogical principles require scaffolding prompts from easy, confidence-building questions to increasingly difficult concepts pitched at the learner's advancing level. Socratic prompting also unlocks latent knowledge through feigned ignorance, avoiding unhelpful blunt answers. These evidence-based techniques improve educational outcomes.

- **Medical:** Strict constraints are required when generating medical suggestions to avoid recommendations lacking established clinical support. Prompts should frame outputs as exploratory hypotheses for experts to vet, not definitive advice, and include citations. Conservative framing is prudent in high-risk domains.

In each case, specialized prompting strategies building on general principles enable unlocking capabilities tuned for domain needs and ethics. Prompting remains as much an art as a science.

Hybrid Approaches

Looking forward, combining learned prompting strategies with structured knowledge offers promising potential to overcome the limitations of both approaches.

For example, chain-of-thought prompting incorporates high-level reasoning frameworks while utilizing LLMs for lower-level generative completions:

1. Decompose complex goals into hierarchical skills and subtasks.
2. Learned classifiers select suitable prompts to complete each subtask.
3. LLM generations provide the required details for the overall structure.
4. Aggregate structured outputs into final coherent wholes.

In this approach, the hierarchical framework mitigates weaknesses in unstructured LLM chaining like losing track of goals. LLMs generate supportive content without requiring unguided long-term coherence.

As another hybrid example, retrieved hard knowledge from databases could ground free-form generative explorations:

1. Start with a structured query to extract key facts.
2. Provide facts to prime the LLM, framing subsequent probing.
3. Allow open-ended speculative continuation tethered to hard data.
4. Evaluate consistency between retrieved knowledge and LLM-generated hypotheses.

By synergistically combining strengths, hybrid approaches transcend limitations of both structured and unstructured systems. However, interface design and workflow integration remain open challenges.

Safety and Ethics

Prompt engineering equips us to steer, though not perfectly control, LLM behaviors. However, full automation, absent transparency and oversight poses risks.

Generating toxic content, plagiarism, and bias persist as concerns. Responsible practices, even for relatively constrained business use cases, include:

1. Monitoring outputs and halting models if red lines are crossed.

2. Constraining context windows to avoid replicating copyrighted training data.
3. Testing for harmful biases with targeted prompts.
4. Seeking and incorporating feedback from impacted communities.
5. Watermarking AI-generated content to avoid confusion.

Avoid automating generative models end-to-end without human checkpoints. While not foolproof, prompt engineering allows channeling capabilities toward beneficial purposes. Still, ethical development needs broader cross-functional governance beyond prompt engineering alone.

Conclusion

Basic single-turn prompting provides only limited utility for advanced reasoning use cases. Chaining prompts, constraining responses, scoring uncertainty, and optimization during deployment offer complementary advances that help overcome inherent LLM limitations like forgetfulness and lack of common sense. Automation further enables leveraging these methods without excessive human involvement.

Continued advances in prompting models, not just foundations, remain critical to delivering robust capabilities aligned with human values. Prompt engineering is a learnable skill that meaningfully impacts real-world applications. Mastering this art accelerates benefits while upholding safety and ethics.

16

TRAINING LLMS

As we learned in Chapter 2, large language models demonstrate remarkable natural language capabilities after extensive training on massive text datasets. However, most business leaders lack perspectives on the intricate process of how these models actually learn from data computationally.

This chapter aims to demystify key concepts, methods, and considerations around training LLMs for leaders exploring adoption but lacking technical specialization.

I will overview critical facets of model development while referring back to previous chapters for foundational context, avoiding duplication. My goal is supporting prudent planning and governance. Let's begin exploring the training pipeline underpinning LLMs' latent potential.

Pre-training Objectives

In Chapter 3, we explored how transformer neural network architectures enable LLMs to comprehend language by representing semantic relationships between words mathematically. However, these networks alone merely provide potential capacity. Models only exhibit practical skills after optimization drives their millions of parameters to encode patterns from training datasets. This dataset exposure occurs in two key phases—pre-training and fine-tuning.

Pre-training is the initial stage where models learn general linguistic knowledge from unlabeled text corpora—essentially any writing like books, news articles or websites. The model processes these texts to understand how language is structured statistically without being tailored to any specific task yet.

Popular pre-training objectives include:

1. Masked language modeling: Randomly masking words in input sentences and having the model predict suitable replacements based on context. This teaches understanding of semantic relationships.

2. Replaced token detection: Identifying words substituted inconsistent with the context. This focuses models on coherence.

3. Sentence reordering: Shuffling sentence order and having models reconstruct logical progressions. This builds awareness of narrative flow.

Pre-training objectives expose models to a diversity of texts to ingest broad language comprehension capabilities and the world knowledge required for downstream tasks.

Architectures

In Chapter 3, we explored transformer architectures that process words in parallel to understand relationships between far apart tokens. Architectural choices impact model capabilities. For instance, decoder-only models produce fluent text but may lack deep reasoning skills. Encoder-only models comprehend language well but may not generate text smoothly. Encoder-decoder models balance both abilities. Larger models also excel but require exponentially more data and compute. Being mindful of these capability tradeoffs allows aligning models to business needs.

Datasets

As highlighted in Chapter 13, the scale and quality of training datasets crucially impact model performance. Malicious actors could potentially poison datasets with toxic patterns that models then inherit. Biases like gender, racial, or ideological skews in data distribution also propagate unless mitigated. However, curating high-quality datasets remains challenging and expensive. Some promising directions include:

1. Synthetic data generation, like back-translating through multiple languages, provides cheap self-supervised training signals. By translating a sentence to another language and then back-translating it, you often end up with a sentence that is slightly different but still semantically similar to the original. This augmented data helps in improving the robustness of models by providing more varied training examples.

2. Leveraging naturally occurring data like online book corpora avoids manually labeling datasets. Public licensing should be verified.

3. Seeking diverse community feedback helps surface harmful biases and remove sensitive examples early. Ongoing participation is ideal.

Overall, the data itself warrants even more scrutiny than models during development. Data contains implicit values, biases and consent issues easily overlooked. Establishing an ethical data supply chain is fundamental but difficult work requiring persistent collaboration between technical practitioners, domain experts, and impacted communities.

Compute Infrastructure

In Chapter 9, we explored the staggering computational requirements of training modern LLMs. Specialized hardware accelerators like GPUs and TPUs are essential for feasibility given the quadrillions of arithmetic operations involved in tuning billions of parameters on trillion-token datasets. Accessing enough processing capacity remains challenging for smaller organizations lacking massive data centers. Some helpful strategies include:

- Optimizing data and model parallelism to distribute workload across available hardware efficiently.
- Leveraging cloud computing vendors to run limited training experiments before investing in infrastructure.
- Exploring collaborations with research entities having access to advanced computing resources.

- Seeking grants, credits and incentives from vendors and governments to increase accessibility.
- Carefully evaluating carbon emissions and sustainability tradeoffs when planning training projects.

With deliberate optimization and partnerships, the benefits of LLMs need not be gated to only hyper-scale entities. But computational demands remain a key challenge requiring informed resource planning.

Training Process

The training process exposes models to datasets iteratively to tune parameters incrementally. Each cycle involves four key steps:

1. Passing input data like text sequences into the model.
2. Having the model process the inputs and make predictions.
3. Quantifying prediction errors compared to the desired training objectives.
4. Adjusting model parameters slightly to reduce errors.

Repeating these four steps hundreds of times cycles through the entire dataset, incrementally improving parameters to minimize objective errors.

Additional techniques that enable stable convergence include:

Cyclical learning rates: Imagine you're trying to find the lowest point in a hilly landscape while blindfolded. At first, you might take big steps to move down quickly, but as you get closer to the lowest point, you take smaller steps to find the exact location carefully. Cyclical learning rates work in a similar way; they adjust the size of the steps the model takes to find the best solution, ensuring it doesn't miss or overshoot the target.

Gradient clipping: Think of a car's speed limiter that prevents it from going too fast for safety. Gradient clipping does something similar for our model; if it's making changes too rapidly, which could be harmful, gradient clipping ensures it doesn't exceed a safe speed, leading to a smoother and safer learning journey.

Regularization: Suppose you're teaching someone to hit a golf ball. If they focus too much on the last swing they saw, they might struggle when conditions change. Regularization ensures the model doesn't pay too much attention to any specific example but learns more general rules, making it adaptable to new situations.

Versioning data pipelines, models, experiments and results is also essential for reproducibility, accountability and production readiness. Training rigor separates robust models from precarious overfits.

Training Procedures

Standard training procedures aim for optimal model performance on metrics. However, as discussed in Chapter 14, solely chasing metrics risks overlooking human values. For instance, blindness to demographic biases could emerge despite strong overall results. Some promising directions to impart social awareness include:

- Reinforcement Learning from Human Feedback[48]: Having models interact with real users and incrementally improve based on feedback ratings on attributes like helpfulness, harmlessness, and honesty.

- Constitutional AI[46]: Recursively editing model outputs to conform to principles of honesty, empathy and harmlessness.

- Value learning[47]: Optimizing directly for avoiding harmful stereotypes and exhibiting pro-social behavior.

Overall, effective training requires a holistic definition of performance exceeding narrow metrics to include ethical alignment. But translating principles into procedures remains technically and philosophically challenging. Responsible progress demands perseverance on both technical and ethical fronts simultaneously.

Fine-Tuning

After pre-training to learn general knowledge, models then fine-tune on smaller labeled datasets to specialize for specific tasks. For instance, a generative writing assistant would fine-tune on domain-specific documents such as existing marketing collateral and product descriptions. This stage is crucial for adapting pre-trained foundations to business needs, often dramatically boosting performance compared to training custom models from scratch.

Two promising fine-tuning techniques include prompt-based training and intermediate task training.

Prompt-based training:

Rather than input-output examples, models learn from prompts that demonstrate the task, like summarizing product brochures. Humans then give feedback.

Intermediate task training:

Intermediate task training[48] is a technique that helps prevent overfitting during fine-tuning. Overfitting means the model becomes too narrowly specialized, like memorizing training examples rather than learning general skills.

Intermediate task training helps avoid this by doing the fine-tuning in two stages:

1. First, the early layers of the model are trained on a large general dataset for an intermediary task. This teaches the model broad linguistic skills.

2. Then, the later layers of the model are trained for the final specialized task, like summarizing legal documents.

Breaking fine-tuning into two steps means the early layers retain general knowledge from the large intermediate dataset rather than overly specializing for the final task.

This prevents overfitting because the model keeps a foundation of broad language skills gained during intermediate task training. The two-stage approach helps balance generalization and specialization for the best performance.

Careful fine-tuning unlocks immense value from foundation models. But solely chasing metrics risks misalignment, necessitating holistic human oversight.

Catastrophic Forgetting

Early attempts to fine-tune massive pre-trained models like GPT-3 on modest target datasets encountered catastrophic forgetting. Updating all parameters causes specialization for the niche dataset to override original knowledge. Performance on benchmarks used during pre-training then plummets as core competencies are lost.

Imagine a chemistry journal article generation model fine-tuned on a small dataset of chemistry abstracts. It becomes highly proficient at producing abstracts, but loses the ability to discuss broader topics like politics, movies or philosophy covered during pre-training.

Catastrophic forgetting poses barriers to safely tapping into the broad capacity of large models. Ongoing research aims to enable fine-tuning that augments capabilities without degrading the general knowledge learned over months of pre-training.

Parameter Efficient Fine-Tuning

Parameter efficient fine-tuning[49] (PEFT) methods like LoRA[50] (Low Rank Adaptation) identify a small subset of parameters to update during tuning. This prevents disrupting the vast majority of parameters encoding general knowledge accumulated during pre-training.

For example, LoRA may only tune 0.5-2% of the overall parameters when specializing a model for a particular domain or dataset. The remaining 97-99.5% of the original model parameters remain frozen. This avoids catastrophic forgetting of capabilities learned during pre-training.

By limiting tuning to critical parameters based on attention and gradient analysis, PEFT sustainably taps into the broad capacity of large models without attempting disruptive full retraining. We will look into these techniques in more detail in the next chapter.

Efficiency Benefits

Besides mitigating catastrophic forgetting, PEFT confers enormous efficiency benefits. Full fine-tuning activates the entire model during training, which is infeasible for models with hundreds of millions of parameters or more.

PEFT methods like LoRA freeze most parameters, only running the small tuned set at high precision needed for training. This significantly reduces memory and compute requirements.

Quantization is another technique that reduces the precision of parameters. It's about simplifying the numbers a model uses. Instead of using very detailed numbers (like 32-bit floating point numbers), quantization means we'll use simpler, shorter numbers (like 8-bit numbers). This is a bit like rounding up prices to the nearest dollar instead of counting cents. The advantage? It uses less memory and speeds up calculations, making it cheaper and faster to run the model. But, like using a limited palette, there's a trade-off: you lose a bit of detail. However, with the right tech-

niques, the impact on the model's performance can be
minimal.

So, PEFT techniques combined with quantization slashes
resource demands while avoiding catastrophic forgetting.
This unlocks practical fine-tuning of vast yet efficient LLM
capabilities on typical hardware. But fully quantizing down
to 8-bits also enables optimized deployment after specialization.

Multi-Task Models

Rather than fine-tuning a separate model for each specialized application, multi-task learning[51] exposes a single
model to diverse datasets and objectives simultaneously
during training.

For example, consider a sales assistant application that
needs to exhibit three key skills:

1. Fluency in natural conversation to engage
   customers.
2. Deep knowledge of the company's products and
   services.
3. Ability to qualify leads and identify promising
   opportunities.

A standard approach would involve fine-tuning three separate models, each trained exclusively on data for a single
skill. However, multi-task learning offers an alternative
strategy.

With multi-task learning, a single model is trained in parallel
on data spanning all three skills. The model learns conversa-

tion from open-domain dialogue datasets, gains product expertise from catalogs and documentation, and develops lead qualification abilities using examples of tagged interactions.

This joint training across diverse objectives better resembles how humans learn transferable skills. Exposing the model to a blend of datasets grants versatility exceeding narrow specialization.

However, care is needed in the training process. If one objective dominates the training signal, it risks overpowering other skills. For example, abundant conversational data may impair specialized product knowledge.

Meticulous tuning of batch sizes, loss weightings, and introduction order minimizes such negative interactions between datasets and skills. With sufficient data quality and compute resources, multi-task models exhibit remarkable generalization capabilities.

So rather than myopically overfitting to individual domains, multi-task learning grants models adaptable breadth similar to human expertise. However, successfully balancing performance across many tasks remains technically challenging. When thoughtfully orchestrated, multi-task training unlocks versatile and transferable LLMs aligned with diverse business needs.

Unsupervised Fine-Tuning

Most fine-tuning relies on humans labeling data for specific skills. However, emerging unsupervised approaches continue model development post-deployment by harnessing distributional shifts in unlabeled user interaction data.

For example, a medical assistant would learn from clinician feedback and refine diagnosis abilities over time. Or a model fine-tuned to predict edited text generates higher quality initial samples according to human reviews. Unlabeled data offers fertile ground for improving fluency and coherence that complement dataset shortcomings.

However, this risks unpredictable behaviors absent oversight. Carefully engineered human feedback loops remain essential to uphold safety during continuous unsupervised adaptation.

Reinforcement Learning

As discussed above, reinforcement learning from human feedback provides specialized optimization for complex objectives like usefulness, harmlessness, and honesty that prove difficult to supervise directly.

Here, models generate candidate responses, and human preferences provide the training signal to guide policy improvement. For example, by comparing outputs from two models, the superior response can be identified and used to update parameters and optimize results over time.

This allows adapting models dynamically for qualities lacking from static training data. However, care is needed to avoid distorting incentives, like deceptive answers being rewarded for seeming correct. Systematic auditing and iteration best unlock benefits while accounting for risks.

The Path Forward

This overview of model training showcases the intricacies involved in instilling LLMs with knowledge and capabilities surpassing human proficiency on narrow domains. We discussed multi-phase procedures like pre-training, fine-tuning, model selection and synthetic data that enable controlled specialization without catastrophic forgetting.

However, risks related to data quality, training stability, evaluation methodology, and potential harms require diligent monitoring and mitigation practices to ensure real-world reliability and safety at each step. Responsible training is crucial for translating cutting-edge research into solutions benefiting humanity.

Looking ahead, improving computational efficiency, generalizable architectures, principled evaluation and human preference incorporation represent priorities for the field. There are also growing efforts to enhance model quality through advanced training objectives, datasets, architectures, and feedback processes.

LLM training remains resource intensive yet rapidly evolving to shape model behaviors for the broad benefit of society. While progress has been breathtaking, purposefully directing these capabilities toward wisdom and ethics remains a significant challenge for research and deployment.

Understanding the processes that give rise to functionality provides the insight needed to evaluate tradeoffs, set expectations, and ensure prudent oversight by cross-functional leadership teams during adoption.

17

EFFICIENT MODEL FINE-TUNING

Many companies struggle to leverage effectively recent advances like large language models. Challenges include the expense of commercial cloud computing for training and deployment, as well as AI talent scarcity.

As introduced in the previous chapter, emerging techniques for efficient fine-tuning of pre-trained models like LoRA and PEFT aim to lower these barriers. They adapt only a small subset of model weights, drastically reducing compute, data storage, and financial costs.

This chapter provides business leaders with a deep dive of Parameter-Efficient Fine-Tuning techniques, reviewing capabilities and limitations. I examine their potential to expand access to advanced AI amid constraints from Big Tech's dominant ecosystems.

The Escalating Costs of Large AI Models

In recent years, artificial intelligence has been transformed by the rise of large neural network models like GPT-3. But size comes at a cost. As previously covered, training such models can require thousands of GPUs for weeks, costing millions of dollars even for tech giants. For example, training GPT-3 cost an estimated $12 million. Large model checkpoints also require substantial storage, with GPT-3 weighing in at 350GB.

This creates a dilemma for companies looking to tap into the powers of large language models. Accessing commercial API services can be prohibitively expensive at scale and incurs in significant downstream risks due to training data opacity, for example. But training customized models internally is likely infeasible without vast engineering resources. Mid-sized players are stuck in the middle.

Once trained, deploying large models for inference also demands substantial compute. Real-time chatbots and creative applications require powerful GPU servers. As discussed previously, this ongoing expense limits viable business models, often reserved only for Big Tech.

As models continue rapidly scaling up in size, these constraints will only worsen. Even large enterprises struggle to experiment with or productize huge models. Efficiency improvements are necessary to prevent concentration in a few dominant hands.

Promising Techniques for More Efficient Fine-Tuning

In response, researchers have developed new techniques to adapt pre-trained models more efficiently. These include LoRA (Low-Rank Adaptation) and a range of methods grouped under the term PEFT (Parameter-Efficient Fine-Tuning).

Both approaches only update a tiny fraction of model weights when specializing for downstream tasks, keeping the majority frozen. This provides performance nearly on par with full fine-tuning while greatly reducing computational and data storage demands.

We'll cover the key capabilities and limitations of LoRA and PEFT shortly. But first, let's examine why they can run so efficiently compared to full fine-tuning of gigantic models.

Understanding Efficient Fine-Tuning

Large AI models like GPT-3 contain hundreds of billions of parameters. These parameters are the weights that define the model's behavior. Originally, they are randomly initialized. The model is then trained on massive datasets to tune these weights gradually in a process called pre-training.

This pre-trained model can then be fine-tuned to specialize for particular tasks. Conventional fine-tuning updates all weights by continuing training on smaller datasets.

However, researchers realized only a tiny fraction of weights may need updating to adapt well. LoRA and PEFT leverage this insight.

For example, LoRA inserts new trainable matrices that essentially overlay on top of the frozen pre-trained weights. PEFT techniques like prefix tuning only update embeddings for special adapter tokens pre-pended to inputs.

In both cases, nearly all pre-trained weights are frozen. This accounts for their efficiency gains in computation, memory, and disk usage.

Now let's explore LoRA and PEFT specifically in more detail. We'll focus first on LoRA, which has received intense interest for ultra low-resource fine-tuning.

LoRA: Extremely Efficient Fine-Tuning via Low-Rank Adaptation

LoRA stands for Low-Rank Adaptation. It was proposed by researchers at Microsoft and CMU in a 2021 paper[50]. LoRA inserts trainable low rank matrices into a pre-trained model to adapt it for downstream tasks.

Nearly all weights remain frozen. For example, with GPT-3's 175 billion parameters, LoRA may update only 2-4 million—over 10,000x fewer than full fine-tuning. This extreme efficiency makes LoRA intriguing for opening up large AI models.

How LoRA Lowers Computational Requirements

Computational costs for training and inference depend heavily on model size. More weights require proportionally more operations and data movement.

LoRA reduces costs by only updating a tiny fraction of weights, defined by new low-rank matrices added to each layer. For example, GPT-3 may use matrices with rank as low as 1 or 2, adapting only 0.01% of weights.

This directly reduces floating point operations (FLOPs) for training and inference by orders of magnitude. Memory bandwidth needs also shrink drastically.

Together, this cuts hardware requirements for training with LoRA up to 3000x lower than full fine-tuning in terms of

GPUs or TPUs. Commercial cloud costs can decrease proportionally.

In absolute terms, models with hundreds of billions of parameters can potentially be tuned on a single consumer GPU. Demands for specialized data center hardware are reduced.

Lower Storage Requirements

In addition to computational demands, model size also creates bottlenecks around storage. For example, fine-tuned versions of GPT-3 weigh in at 350GB each.

Storing one specialized model per task becomes impractical at this scale. LoRA reduces this burden by only requiring extra storage for the tiny adapted matrices.

For GPT-3, these may occupy just tens of MBs. This allows cheaply maintaining many specialized models simultaneously.

Rapid Task Switching

Together, slashing computational and storage costs allows rapid switching between models adapted for different tasks.

Rather than having to load entirely different 350GB checkpoints, only lightweight matrix parameters need swapping. This makes context switching seamless in real world deployment.

Limitations of LoRA

LoRA offers intriguing possibilities for opening up large language models. But limitations remain. Most critically, LoRA still relies entirely on the pre-trained weights and architecture. Only the introduction of lightweight task matrices is exposed. Unless leveraging open source models, this means reliance on proprietary models like GPT-4, limiting flexibility and increasing risks of lock-in. Open questions also persist around model quality tradeoffs.

Additionally, training still requires access to specialized hardware like GPUs or TPUs, if at reduced scale. Utilizing commercial cloud resources remains the norm.

In essence, LoRA provides an alluring on-ramp for efficient fine-tuning. But the underlying ecosystem remains largely centralized and closed. Next, we'll explore PEFT, which offers complementary strengths and weaknesses.

PEFT: A Collection of Techniques for Parameter Efficient Fine-Tuning

PEFT stands for Parameter-Efficient Fine-Tuning. It refers to an evolving collection of techniques that fine-tune large models by only updating a tiny fraction of weights.

PEFT methods include prefix tuning, prompt tuning, adapter tuning, and bit fitting, among others. They're distinguished from LoRA by exposing some internal weights rather than just adding new matrices on top.

Let's survey some popular PEFT approaches and their capabilities.

1. Prefix Tuning

One interesting PEFT technique is prefix tuning, introduced in 2021. It adds trainable token embeddings to the start of model inputs.

For example, a question might be prefixed with a learned [Query] token. Only embeddings for such special tokens are tuned, leaving underlying weights frozen.

Typically, the number of new embeddings ranges from tens to a few thousand—negligibly small compared to models with hundreds of billions of weights. Compute and storage savings mirror the limited parameter growth.

This method leverages the insight that large models already contain extensive knowledge. A small prompt can guide them to exhibit desired behavior without comprehensive fine-tuning.

2. Bit-Fit

Bit-fit is among the most parameter efficient PEFT methods. It only trains model bias terms, keeping all weights frozen.

Imagine a large orchestra playing a beautiful piece of music. Each musician (representing the "weights" in a model) has their role and knows exactly how to play their part. The conductor (representing the "bias" in Bit-Fit) doesn't change the notes each musician plays but can influence how loudly or softly the orchestra plays, or speed up or slow down the tempo. The conductor's influence can change the overall feel of the music without changing the individual notes.

In the Bit-Fit method, instead of re-teaching every musician in the orchestra a new piece of music (which would be like retraining all the weights), we just provide guidance or a nudge (the bias) to get a different sound or adapt to a new style. This approach is more efficient and requires less effort than teaching every single musician a new piece.

So, "bias" in this context is like the small adjustments or nudges made by the conductor to get the desired performance from the orchestra without changing the core essence of the music.

Since biases represent a minuscule fraction of all weights, this drastically reduces resource demands. For example, bit-fit may adapt as little as 0.01% of weights in huge models.

The tradeoff is limited flexibility compared to other techniques. Since weights are fixed, only output distributions can be rebalanced rather than internal behavior. But the efficiency gains are unmatched.

3. Adapter-Based Methods

Recently, adapter layers have become a popular architecture for parameter efficient tuning. These add small bottleneck layers throughout a model.

Only adapter parameters are trained, freezing the weights of the original model. This provides more flexibility than bit-fit but less than full retraining.

Overall, PEFT offers a spectrum of techniques with varying flexibility and efficiency tradeoffs. Researchers continue innovating new methods at a rapid pace.

Limitations of PEFT

PEFT methods can reduce costs by over 1000x compared to full fine-tuning of gigantic models.

Most techniques only allow limited tuning within the external architecture of proprietary models. Unlike open source code, the core models remain closed. PEFT also invariably relies on commercial cloud infrastructure for training and deployment.

In addition, model quality tradeoffs need further assessment across different domains. More limited parameter updates may hit ceilings depending on inherent task flexibility needs.

Nonetheless, PEFT constitutes an important stepping stone toward democratizing access to capable large models.

Implications for Business Leaders

LoRA and PEFT offer intriguing opportunities for businesses seeking to leverage large language models. Suggestions include:

1. Accelerate experimentation by radically reducing compute and data costs for fine-tuning GPT-4 and others.

2. Customize models for niche internal applications without dependence on expensive cloud APIs.

3. Rapidly switch models on the fly for diverse customer-facing services.

4. Achieve state-of-the-art results with frugal resources by building on leading open source models like LLaMA 2.

5. However, these techniques should be adopted with eyes wide open regarding limitations:

6. Avoid undue dependence on dominant tech players' proprietary pre-trained models. Try mixing with open source models where possible.

7. Recognize that transparency of model weights alone doesn't ensure fair competition or alignment with broad social interests.

8. Develop prudent contingency plans as massive computational scale increasingly becomes a competitive barrier limiting market entry.

Overall, techniques like LoRA and PEFT show encouraging possibilities for expanding access to advanced AI. But true diversification requires addressing concentration of resources like data, compute infrastructure, and AI talent—not just releasing model weights.

18

REINFORCING AI CAPABILITIES
WITH HUMAN FEEDBACK

While LLMs are impressive, there remains a question of alignment: How can these models better adhere to human values, preferences, and needs? The answer might lie in Reinforcement Learning from Human Feedback (RLHF).

The Essence of RLHF

At its core, RLHF is about bridging the gap between machines and humans, bringing AI systems closer to our values and preferences. Traditional model training relies on vast datasets pre-labeled by humans, a cumbersome and sometimes imprecise method. RLHF shakes up this status quo by integrating human feedback directly into the AI training process.

Imagine a pre-trained language model capable of generating a myriad of text snippets in response to a prompt. Instead of solely relying on human-labeled datasets, with RLHF, humans systematically compare and rank these AI-generated responses. These preferences form the foundation of a "reward model." The AI is then optimized using reinforcement learning techniques to favor outputs that score higher on this reward model.

This approach has a significant advantage. Instead of training the model using fixed data, the model evolves based on dynamic, direct human input. As a result, the model can understand intricate, subjective attributes such as creativity, appropriateness, and truthfulness—attributes hard to distill into traditional datasets.

Impact and Significance of RLHF

The advent of RLHF represents a paradigm shift in the AI community. Powerhouses like OpenAI have leaned on this technique to birth advanced chatbot models such as Chat-GPT. The difference in quality is palpable. Instead of merely predicting the next word in a sequence, these models generate content more aligned with our real-world preferences and values.

Yet, the power of RLHF isn't just theoretical. Practical applications are already surfacing. Consider the task of text summarization. Traditionally, AI models for summarization were trained to mimic human-made summaries. However, OpenAI researchers demonstrated[52] that by employing RLHF—having humans compare AI-generated summaries and refining the model based on feedback—the quality of summaries drastically improved. In fact, with enough iterations, the AI-generated summaries even eclipsed their human counterparts in terms of quality.

The power of RLHF isn't confined to text. It opens doors to countless applications—whether it's speech recognition, image generation, or translation. The key lies in the feedback loop. By directly catering to human needs and iteratively refining based on feedback, the model learns to prioritize user satisfaction over mere benchmark achievements.

Challenges in RLHF Implementation

However, RLHF isn't a silver bullet. The technique comes with its share of challenges:

1. **Data Intensiveness:** RLHF is voracious in its demand for data. A constant influx of human feedback is essential, and this can mean significant human labor and associated costs.

2. **Bias and Generalization Issues:** The AI is only as good as the feedback it receives. If evaluators are not well briefed, have biases, or provide inconsistent feedback, the AI can adopt those flaws, sometimes with harmful consequences.

3. **Complex Implementation:** Though promising, RLHF demands vast computational resources, extensive data, and meticulous engineering to scale.

Leading AI research hubs are fully aware of these limitations. As we advance, the focus will be on refining RLHF techniques, developing more efficient algorithms, and devising strategies to minimize potential harms.

19

ENSEMBLE MODELS, MIXTURE OF EXPERTS, AND THE POWER OF COLLABORATION

As with many challenges in business, a multifaceted problem often benefits from diverse solutions. Instead of relying on a single expert model, imagine the outcome when many experts contribute. This chapter not only delves into Ensemble Models and Mixture of Experts (MoE), but also addresses the rising speculations about the use of MoE in GPT-4, which has set the tech world abuzz.

What are Ensemble Models?

Imagine you are in a board meeting, trying to make a crucial decision. Rather than relying solely on one person's perspective, you solicit input from multiple board members. Their collective wisdom often leads to a more informed and holistic decision. Ensemble models work in a similar way.

At its core, an ensemble model combines predictions from several models to deliver a final decision. Instead of relying on the output of a single model, the ensemble leverages the strengths of each member model, mitigating individual model weaknesses.

Benefits:

1. Risk Diversification: Similar to diversifying an investment portfolio, ensemble models mitigate the risk of any single model's poor performance.

2. Improved Accuracy: Collectively, the predictions of multiple models tend to be more accurate than any individual prediction.

3. Versatility: Different models might have specialties. By combining them, you benefit from diverse areas of expertise.

While LLMs like GPT have set the benchmark high, ensemble techniques can push the boundaries even further.

Mixture of Experts: A Division of Labor

With the latest rumors suggesting that GPT-4 might employ an advanced Mixture of Experts technique, it's crucial to dissect this concept and understand its implications for businesses. If ensemble models are akin to board members contributing collectively, then the MoE can be likened to a team where each member has a unique skill set.

Unlike traditional AI systems that use a uniform model for all inputs, MoE segregates tasks among multiple "expert" models, each possessing unique parameters. An expert selector systematically picks the most apt experts based on the input type, activating only a sparse subset of the overall parameters. This sparse activation allows MoE models to accommodate a vastly higher number of parameters without excessively amplifying computational demands.

For language-related tasks, distinct experts specialize in diverse areas. For instance, while one expert is attuned to the intricacies of grammar, another is well-versed in factual knowledge. Such specialization ensures that the nuances of natural language are adeptly handled, with each word or phrase being routed to the optimal expert or combination of experts.

A noteworthy attribute of MoE is its scalability while retaining efficiency. Although a MoE model might encompass trillions of parameters, only a minuscule portion is employed for any given input.

Groundbreaking Implementation of MoE in Language AI

Though MoE's foundational idea isn't new, recent advances in model parallelism and distributed training have renewed interest in its application, especially in large language models.

Some pivotal projects showcasing the potential of MoE include:

1. Switch Transformers[61]: This method streamlines MoE routing strategies. In experiments, it has been observed to accelerate training by up to 8x compared to dense models, thanks to its intelligent computation allocation.

2. GLaM (Google's Large Model)[62]: With a staggering 1.2 trillion parameters, GLaM uses MoE to attain superior performance. Even with just 8% of its parameters active during any task, it significantly outshines models like the 175 billion parameter GPT-3 across various language benchmarks.

These projects underscore the remarkable leaps MoE offers in model capacity, capability, and efficiency. If the rumors hold true, and GPT-4 indeed incorporates MoE, hitting the 1+ trillion parameter mark, it shows OpenAI's innovative strategies that surmount scaling challenges.

Benefits:

1. Efficiency and Speed: Specialized components can process their domains much quicker, allowing for faster decisions.

2. Resource Allocation: In a business environment where resources (like computational power) are limited, allocating specific tasks to specialized models ensures maximum efficiency.

3. Tailored Solutions: For complex problems that involve various domains, MoEs can deliver nuanced solutions that take into account all facets of the issue.

While the specifics about GPT-4's architecture are yet to be unveiled, its potential scale showcases the vast possibilities and challenges that MoE presents in language AI.

Bridging with LLM Training

In my earlier chapter on training LLMs, I established that models undergo intensive training, learning from vast amounts of data, and iterating upon their mistakes. Now, let's place ensemble and MoE models in the context of this training:

1. **Fine-tuning with Ensembles**: Post the general pre-training phase of a LLM, multiple models could be fine-tuned using different subsets of data or varied techniques.

The collective predictions of these fine-tuned models can enhance task-specific performance.

2. Introducing Expertise in Training: When training a MoE model, each expert can be thought of as undergoing its specialized training regimen. They hone their expertise based on specific portions of the training data most relevant to them.

3. Continuous Learning and Adaptation: Ensemble and MoE models, like LLMs, benefit from continuous feedback. As each model (or expert) iterates and improves, the collective system becomes more robust and resilient.

Implications for Business Strategy

Resource Planning: Implementing ensemble models or MoE might require more computational resources upfront. However, the long-term payoffs in terms of efficiency, speed, and accuracy can be worth the investment.

Flexibility: Ensemble and MoE systems can be more adaptable to changing business landscapes. If one model becomes outdated, it can be replaced or updated without overhauling the entire system.

Conclusion

The realms of ensemble models and mixtures of experts offer promising avenues for businesses looking to leverage the power of LLMs. As with any tool, their efficacy is determined not just by their technical prowess, but by how leaders strategically deploy, monitor, and refine them. In the ever-evolving landscape of AI, these methods provide yet another testament to the age-old belief: there's strength in numbers.

LLM-ENABLED APPLICATIONS: AREAS OF RESEARCH AND INNOVATION

The research and advancement of large language models have surged, delivering innovations that have started to redefine the capabilities of Artificial Intelligence. New platforms like LangChain provide flexible abstractions and extensive toolkits, enabling businesses to deliver LLM-powered applications. Here, I distill three primary areas of research and innovation that business leaders should monitor closely.

Retrieval-Augmented Generation (RAG)

RAG[15] is the fusion of parametric neural networks (the typical structure of AI models) with non-parametric memories (large external knowledge bases). By combining these two elements, AI systems gain the capacity to retrieve and incorporate external knowledge when generating text, thus producing more accurate and informed outputs.

How it works:

- A user provides a text input, which could be a question or a prompt.
- A neural retriever queries a vast knowledge base, like a corporate database, to find pertinent information.
- The retrieved data then informs the text generator, which uses both the original input and this data to produce a knowledgeable and accurate response.

Business Implications:

RAG has the potential to revolutionize many sectors by bringing more informative AI insights. Executives could receive synthesized briefings on industry news, customer service could offer more accurate answers, and knowledge workers might gain a significant boost in productivity. The ability to update the external memory also ensures the AI remains current with global changes.

Challenges:

Further research is needed to refine RAG's deployment across different settings and to improve its reasoning capabilities.

Program-Aided Language Models (PAL)

PAL[17] addresses the challenge that large language models, despite their impressive language generation skills, often falter in precise mathematical reasoning. This technique blends neural networks with symbolic programming to ensure robust reasoning.

How it works:

- Instead of just generating text-based reasoning, PAL produces reasoning steps as short Python code (or other programming languages).
- These code snippets are then executed in a Python interpreter, ensuring precise mathematical outcomes.

Business Implications:

Businesses relying on quantitative reasoning can gain enhanced reliability using PAL. For sectors that require exact arithmetic execution, PAL provides a more trustworthy solution.

Challenges:

While the hybrid nature of PAL offers many benefits, integrating neural networks with symbolic programming presents coordination challenges. Perfecting this synergy is crucial for achieving robust AI reasoning.

ReAct: Reasoning with Actions

ReAct[53] is a technique that seeks to enhance the accuracy of AI decision-making by interleaving reasoning with real-world actions.

How it works:

- The system undertakes a real-world action, like querying a database.
- It then reasons based on the retrieved data.
- Depending on the gaps identified in its reasoning, it determines subsequent actions.

- This process continues until a conclusion is reached, with every step anchored in real-world data.

Business Implications:

ReAct suggests a paradigm shift in AI reasoning. By mandating that every decision the system makes is grounded in real-world data, businesses can expect more rational and accurate insights from their AI systems.

Challenges:

As with other hybrid models, combining diverse AI techniques into a seamless workflow remains a challenge. However, the benefits of an AI system that is both articulate and accurate in its reasoning make the pursuit worthwhile.

Conclusion

As AI continues its rapid evolution, the path forward seems increasingly to lie in hybrid systems. These innovations—RAG, PAL, and ReAct—are emblematic of this trend, melding traditional neural network strengths with other methods to push AI's capabilities further. For business leaders, an understanding of these advancements isn't just beneficial; it's essential for staying ahead in the AI-driven future.

ETHICAL DEPLOYMENT OF LARGE LANGUAGE MODELS

The rapid pace of progress in AI often leaves society reacting to technological change rather than proactively shaping it. However, the current hype cycle need not imply we fail to determine wise paths forward, benefiting humanity holistically.

While LLMs promise to revolutionize areas ranging from education to healthcare, these models also bear the risk of harmful biases, factual inaccuracies, and inconsistencies that could lead to significant real-world implications. At the same time, completely forsaking such groundbreaking technology would deprive society of many potential benefits.

In this closing chapter, I outline pragmatic recommendations for addressing safety issues through critical testing, data sourcing transparency, monitoring deployment impacts, soliciting wide feedback, and aligning development incentives with ethical priorities. Nuanced solutions balancing risks and opportunities will further collective wellbeing.

Potential Harms

If deployed carelessly into impactful applications, LLMs risk contributing to or amplifying existing societal harms. Generated misinformation could strengthen worrying trends toward truth decay. Factual inaccuracy leads to dangerous errors in high-stakes domains like science and medicine. Repurposing copyrighted material without consent impacts the livelihoods of creators. Toxic or biased text reinforces discrimination and reduces belonging. Unvetted conversational advice directs vulnerable populations astray. And misaligned objectives could scale harassment, radicalization and more through social media. Let's explore some of these risks in more detail:

- **Centralized Control:** Unchecked LLM development may concentrate power among select corporations, institutions, and governments. Most can't assess let alone shape opaque technocratic systems dictating life experience. Passivity enables control by automation. We must establish collective agency in determining ethical technological possibilities benefiting humanity holistically.

- **Truth Decay:** Widespread synthetic media paired with limited critical thinking magnifies risks of "reality apathy" where convenience outweighs truth. Hyper-personalized information bubbles could fragment shared understanding. LLMs could automate mass manipulation were they solely optimized for engagement and profit. Grounding technology in service of wisdom provides our escape route.

- **Intensified Inequity**: LLMs could scale inequalities and bias absent earnest commitment to fair multi-stakeholder participation. Those already advantaged gain more knowledge, creativity, and productivity, compounding gaps. Voices outside privileged communities go unheard and unserved. Progress defined by narrow benchmarks inevitably oppresses. We must widen prosperity through moral imagination.

- **Dehumanization**: Thoughtless over-reliance on deterministic models and metrics erodes human dignity. People become data sources oppressed by algorithms, decreeing truth arbitrarily. Efficiency displaces meaning when technique trumps ethics. But we remain free to affirm values and purpose.

- **Technological Potentiation**: Dual-use risks warrant heightened concern as LLMs grow more capable and accessible. Automating phishing, impersonation, misinformation, harassment, and hacking could catastrophically impact lives absent careful controls and ethics. We aren't helpless given dangers, but nor can we afford naïve innocence.

LLMs don't inherently embody beneficial values absent intentional efforts. They propagate patterns—good and evil—from training data. While scaling can attenuate some issues, progress remains largely measured on convenience metrics like perplexity rather than real-world harm reduction. Without re-orienting development, potential damages may grow in scale alongside capabilities.

Given the stakes involved, responsible LLM development demands judiciousness, not alarmism or indifference. LLMs represent one of the most promising technologies for furthering human knowledge, creativity, and opportunity ever discovered. Realizing benefits ethically while addressing acute challenges merits nuanced open-minded inquiry.

I recommend harm mitigation through ethical and transparent data sourcing, pragmatic testing, monitoring real-world impacts, soliciting wide public feedback, engaging governance, auditing data/systems, thoughtful deployment framing, and user empowerment. Done concertedly, a combination of technical and social safeguards provides a measured path to maximize benefit while preventing harms.

Rigorous Testing

Confidently assessing LLMs requires rigorous empirical testing beyond convenience benchmarks. Protocol suites specifically probing safety, ethics, and broader social impacts would uncover failure modes and inform mitigations. Testing methodologies should draw on interdisciplinary expertise in social psychology, ethics, law, and humanities alongside technical fields. Tests also demand representative human assessment across demographics.

The current benchmarks disproportionately reward scalable dangers. Progress metrics warrant re-orientation toward holistic human values assessment, not optimizations disconnected from ethical priorities. Testing rigor complements technical mitigations and governance by grounding discussion in empirical data.

Monitoring Deployments

Real-time monitoring provides invaluable data on how LLMs perform in practice when deployed publicly. Rule-based classifiers can detect emerging issues and prompt human review. User reporting further surfaces concerns through channels protecting privacy and dignity. Continuous monitoring in production closes the loop between testing and deployment, enabling rapid detection and response to unanticipated issues.

However, solely algorithmic monitoring risks normalizing social harms if statistical patterns reflecting harm are propagated rather than detected as problems. Monitoring demands continuous recalibration based on solicited human perspectives across impacted groups. Maintaining channels for marginalized voices counteracts blind spots emerging from privilege. The goal is expanding awareness, not automation for its own sake.

While continuous monitoring of LLM deployments is crucial for tracking their real-world performance and potential missteps, it presents its own set of ethical challenges. One of the paramount concerns is the preservation of user privacy. In our digital age, monitoring systems can inadvertently capture sensitive user information, leading to potential breaches of confidentiality and unintended data misuse. Such breaches not only violate the trust users place in these platforms but also expose them to various risks, ranging from identity theft to unauthorized profiling.

Moreover, the data storage mechanisms associated with monitoring must be foolproof, ensuring that user data is not vulnerable to external cyber-attacks or internal misuse.

Balancing the need for effective monitoring with these
ethical imperatives requires meticulous planning, robust
data handling practices, and transparent communication
with users about how their data is used and protected.

Seeking Wide Feedback

Developing LLMs responsibly requires earnest engagement
with diverse public voices to represent pluralistic interests,
experiences, and concerns. The temptation to optimize
narrowly for locking in users must be counterbalanced with
active solicitation of feedback from populations easily overlooked by corporations. Intentional, repeated outreach
across languages, geographies, disciplines and social posi-
tions is needed to perceive blind spots.

No group has the monopoly on wisdom—breakthrough
insights on aligning LLMs with human values may come
from unanticipated people and contexts. Well-structured
deliberative processes grounded in ethics, rather than
consolidated authority or narrow voting, provide proper
discernment of the common good. Leaving difficult conversations for later heightens preventable harms.

Incentive Audits

Organizational incentives greatly impact how companies
develop and deploy LLMs in practice, often overwhelming
abstract mission statements. Analyzing training objectives,
benchmark selection, metrics definitions, promotion crite-
ria, product management frameworks and similar concrete
details illuminates where alignment with ethics has—or has

not—been operationalized into everyday work. Incentive audits institutionalize moral incentives.

Findings should inform escalating governance and certifications for LLM development/deployment based on analyzed organizational practices, not just pledged principles or commitments. Policy based on empirical assessment of lived incentives helps prevent unintended harms before they occur.

Auditing for Representation

In developing ethical LLMs, a critical need often overlooked is diversity auditing of training datasets and model outputs. As research from groups like the Distributed AI Research Institute[54] (DAIR) has revealed, sole reliance on technical metrics can mask issues around representation biases.

Proactive auditing through critical analysis of dataset composition and model performance across subgroups makes implicit imbalances explicit. Key dimensions warranting audits include:

• Gender identities

• Race and ethnicities

• Nationalities and cultural backgrounds

• Age groups

• Disabilities

• Neurodiversity

• Socioeconomic status

- Geographic regions

- Religious diversity

- Psychographic segments

- Sensitive demographic attributes

Ideally, both training datasets and models should exhibit fair representation across traditionally marginalized dimensions. However, determining sufficiency remains challenging.

Appropriate auditing requires the involvement of impacted communities beyond sole reliance on internal technical teams. Progress necessitates embracing discomfort over difficult conversations on inequality led by historically unheard voices.

Prioritizing representation audits makes addressing exclusion and correcting imbalances an obligatory aspect of ethical model development, not an optional consideration. Proactive transparency and accountability should match the scale of societal influence these technologies exert. Though the work is hard, the alternative damages us all.

Empowering Users

LLM capabilities hinge on effective human prompting—retaining user agency is both ethically prudent and pragmatically essential. Interfaces should provide visibility into model limitations, confidence scores, training data, and mitigations applied. Users deserve contextual awareness to assess reliability and determine appropriate reliance.

Descriptions should highlight that LLMs are fallible tools, not oracles or conscious agents. Empowered users represent the front line of monitoring for potential harms.

Transparent interfaces also allow advanced users to refine prompts to steer model behavior. Preferences like avoiding toxicity or errors can be encoded. User empowerment sustains ethical human oversight while benefiting from algorithmic assistance. Finding this balance prevents harms of both unchecked automation and total abdication.

Rigorous Documentation

Analogous to how consumer products come equipped with meticulous labels listing their ingredients and intended functionalities, it is imperative that datasets and models are accompanied by exhaustive documentation. This detailed literature should explain every aspect, from their inception and inherent biases to their designated use-cases, limitations, and possible adverse consequences.

The tech community, recognizing this need, has proactively put forth an array of notable frameworks over the past few years to bolster transparency in the realm of machine learning:

1. **Datasheets for Datasets**[41]: As previously discussed, this initiative was conceptualized to bring a standardized format to the information accompanying datasets. Comprehensive datasheets shed light on various facets, ranging from the methodologies employed in data collection to its envisaged usage, its distribution patterns, and potential biases that might taint the data. Such intricate documentation paves the way for developers and end-users alike to gain a

nuanced comprehension of the dataset's merits and demerits.

2. Model Cards for Model Reporting[40]: As previously discussed, Model Cards serve as an informative dossier outlining a model's performance indicators, its training regimen, the data used for evaluation, along with any ethical considerations that arise. These cards function similarly to nutritional information on food products, offering a concise yet thorough overview of the model's potential and constraints.

3. Factsheets[56]: Factsheets build upon the foundation laid by Datasheets. They are tailored specifically to champion transparency in the provision of AI services. They furnish a meticulous dissection of a system's architecture, its training and testing phases, performance metrics, safety protocols, and updates.

4. Data Statements for Natural Language Processing[57]: These statements underscore the importance of understanding the sociocultural landscape, demographic indicators, and the interactive milieu in which data crystallizes. Such insights empower developers and users to navigate the latent assumptions and prejudices entrenched in NLP frameworks.

5. Nutritional Labels for Data and Models[58]: Drawing an analogy to nutritional labels we find on food items, these labels furnish a cursory yet insightful view into the "health metrics" and intricate "composition" of a dataset or model. These aids are instrumental in guiding stakeholders to gauge the caliber, equitability, and lurking hazards of data or computational models.

6. Data Nutrition Project[59, 60]: This endeavor focuses on introducing a standardized rubric that demystifies dataset constituents, their origins, and the spectrum of their viable applications. The overarching ambition is to ensure the datasets that serve as the lifeblood for AI systems are not just technically sound but are also leveraged with a sense of responsibility.

While each of these frameworks boasts unique attributes, they converge on a shared mission: to render the inner workings of LLMs transparent, user-friendly, and amenable to scrutiny.

Comprehensive documentation confers manifold benefits:

- **For Developers:** It gives them a granular understanding of the datasets and models at their disposal, strengthening their decision-making processes and aiding in the creation of superior ethical systems.

- **For End Users:** It offers them insights into the model's operational blueprint, its strengths, and weaknesses, thus facilitating judicious and secure application.

- **For Regulatory Entities:** It grants them access to a treasure trove of critical data, empowering them to draft informed guidelines concerning the stewardship and governance of emerging technologies.

- **For the Global Citizen:** It instills a sense of trust in these cutting-edge technologies, derived from the knowledge that system's evolution is marked by transparency and ethical considerations.

To encapsulate, as LLMs burgeon and permeate diverse sectors, the mandate for transparency, facilitated by all-encompassing documentation, becomes even more pressing.

Policy, Governance and Regulation

Realizing beneficial futures requires purposeful, ethical policies steering technology to uplift humanity. Governance processes should center impacted communities through participatory processes and moral deliberation. Regulations must constrain dangers without stifling innovation. A comprehensive policy toolkit can positively shape progress.

Safety and Oversight Boards

Expert advisory boards provide continuous input based on specialized knowledge of machine learning, law, ethics, social science, and humanities. Oversight boards auditing practices instill accountability. Diverse representation prevents narrow interests from skewing guidance. Collective oversight enacts ethics.

Public Consultation

Policies only sustain legitimacy through inclusive public participation. Wide comment solicitation, independent surveys, citizen assemblies, and grassroots dialogue mean-ingfully represent diverse needs and views. Labor should have equal input to industry. Providing avenues for airing concerns and shaping decisions makes public interests paramount.

Regulatory Standards

Reasonable regulations on safety, quality, fairness, and security guide technology to benefit humanity. Standards enact ethics through mandates rather than hoping for voluntary compliance. However, care is needed to iterate pragmatically without concentrating control or freezing innovation. Striking balances remains challenging but necessary.

Certification Requirements

Trust in AI increases when providers demonstrate ethical practices through external audits. Certifications confirming safety testing, monitoring, mitigations, and redress mechanisms offer assurance to users and communities. Governments can accelerate certification by subsidizing audits for organizations committing to transparency. Market incentives thus scale ethics.

Our policy ecosystem must uphold moral human values and dignity as guiding lights. No single solution is sufficient given multifaceted challenges and uncertainties. Holistic toolkits combining distributed oversight, expert guidance, public consultation, thoughtful regulation, and trusted certifications incentivize ethics and safety. Global cooperation amplifies protections scaling alongside capability growth.

The Path Forward

Addressing complex technology challenges with many unknowns is daunting. However, prudent precautions provide a reasonable path forward: rigorous testing provides empirical grounding; monitoring illuminates issues arising in practice; wide feedback offers representative discernment; incentives audits encourage preventative governance; and user empowerment maintains human oversight. Imperfect but honest efforts maximizing available knowledge supports beneficial progress.

How Business Leaders Avoid Potential Pitfalls

While the recommendations outlined offer constructive starting points, implementing them effectively remains nontrivial. Here are some potential pitfalls that warrant awareness:

1. Performative rather than substantive ethics. Superficial compliance with minimal viable effort rather than earnest commitment. Values must be embedded deeply.

2. Self-assessment rather than external audits. Over-reliance on internal evaluations creates blind spots. Independent scrutiny enables objectivity.

3. Testing on narrow benchmarks. Convenience metrics fail to capture complex socio-technical subtleties. Holistic, human-centered assessments are needed.

4. Limited diversity. Failure to represent marginalized populations and non-mainstream viewpoints adequately. Inclusion is crucial.

5. Myopic monitoring. Focusing on immediate metrics while ignoring long-term implications.

6. User dark patterns. Interfaces that preserve visibility in name only while guiding users towards predetermined outcomes. True empowerment requires ceding some control.

6. Ethics washing. Portraying granular tweaks as comprehensive solutions. Holistic re-alignment is needed beyond isolated mitigations.

Call for Moral Courage

Adapting responsibly to AI's transformation of nearly every sphere of human activity constitutes an immense but essential challenge. Pausing progress relinquishes benefits improving lives, but unfettered acceleration risks potential dangers. Upholding ethics amidst emerging capabilities, hype, and market pressures requires moral courage.

LLMs represent some of the most promising yet ethically fraught technologies ever conceived. Their development plots a razor's edge between utopian and dystopian potentials depending on our choices moving forward.

The road ahead remains opaque, but the first step starts with education of what LLMs are and are not. Only then can leaders make informed decisions away from hype and commercial realities. Progress depends on our choices daily, and the time is now for you to create the world you wish to see.

Stay human!

Inês

Note: Consider leaving a review and sharing the book with others that may benefit from its content.

I encourage you to dive deeper into the technology powering generative AI by reviewing the books and courses on the next page.

KEEP LEARNING

Our books

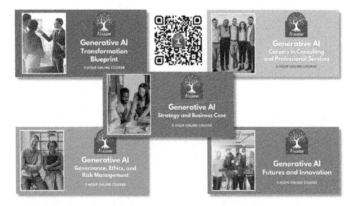

Our courses

ENDNOTES

1. Word2Vec: Google Code Archive

2. Attention Is All You Need by Ashish Vaswani, Noam Shazeer, et al.

3. On the Opportunities and Risks of Foundation Models by Rishi Bommasani, Drew A. Hudson, et al.

4. BloombergGPT: A Large Language Model for Finance by Shijie Wu, Ozan Irsoy, et al.

5. Constitutional AI: Harmlessness from AI Feedback by Yuntao Bai, Saurav Kadavath, et al.

6. Llama 2: Open Foundation and Fine-Tuned Chat Models by Hugo Touvron, Louis Martin, et al.

7. InternetLab: Drag queens and Artificial Intelligence: should computers decide what is 'toxic' on the internet? by Alessandra Gomes, Dennys Antonialli and Thiago Oliva.

8. Meta AI: Galactica: A Large Language Model for Science by Ross Taylor, Marcin Kardas, et al.

9. MIT Technology Review: Why Meta's latest large language model survived only three days online by Will Douglas Heaven.

10. Cleaning up a baby peacock sullied by a non-information spill by Prof. Emily M. Bender

11. GitHub: Novel AI Tokenizer

12. OpenAI: Language Models are Few-Shot Learners by Tom B. Brown, Benjamin Mann, et al.

13. Google: BERT: Pre-training of Deep Bidirectional Transformers for Language Understanding by Jacob Devlin, Ming-Wei Chang, et al.

14. Wired: The Fanfic Sex Trope That Caught a Plundering AI Red-Handed by Rose Eveleth.

15. Retrieval-Augmented Generation for Knowledge-Intensive NLP Tasks by Patrick Lewis, Ethan Perez, et al.

16. Symbolic Knowledge Distillation: from General Language Models to Commonsense Models by Peter West, Chandra Bhagavatula, et al.

17. PAL: Program-aided Language Models by Luyu Gao, Aman Madaan, et al.

18. McKinsey: Unleashing developer productivity with generative AI by Begum Karaci Deniz, Chandra Gnanasambandam, et al.

19. The Verge: Microsoft, GitHub, and OpenAI ask court to throw out AI copyright lawsuit by Emma Roth.

20. The Atlantic: Revealed: The Authors Whose Pirated Books are Powering Generative AI by Alex Reisner.

21. On the Dangers of Stochastic Parrots: Can Language Models Be Too Big? by Emily M. Bender, Timnit Gebru, et al.

22. Generative AI at Work by Erik Brynjolfsson, Danielle Li, and Lindsey Raymond.

23. MIT: Experimental Evidence on the Productivity Effects of Generative Artificial Intelligence by Shakked Noy and Whitney Zhang.

24. The Impact of AI on Developer Productivity: Evidence from GitHub Copilot by Sida Peng, Eirini Kalliamvakou, Peter Cihon, and Mert Demirer.

25. Measuring Human-Automation Function Allocation by Amy R. Pritchett, So Young Kim, and Karen M. Feigh.

26. Harvard Business Review: The Tragic Crash of Flight AF447 Shows the Unlikely but Catastrophic Consequences of Automation by Nick Oliver, Thomas Calvard, and Kristina Potočnik.

27. Falling Asleep at the Wheel: Human/AI Collaboration in a Field Experiment on HR Recruiters by Fabrizio Dell'Acqua

28. Super Mario Meets AI: Experimental Effects of Automation and Skills on Team Performance and Coordination by Fabrizio Dell'Acqua, Bruce Kogut, and Patryk Perkowski.

30. Andreessen Horowitz: Navigating the High Cost of AI Compute by Guido Appenzeller, Matt Bornstein, and Martin Casado.

31. Google "We Have No Moat, And Neither Does OpenAI" by Dylan Patel and Afzal Ahmad.

32. Databricks: Free Dolly: Introducing the World's First Truly Open Instruction-Tuned LLM by Mike Conover, Matt Hayes, et al.

33. Human Redundancy in Automation Monitoring: Effects of Social Loafing and Social Compensation by Juliane Domeinski, Ruth Wagner, et al.

34. The AI compute shortage explained by Nvidia, Crusoe, & MosaicML by Veronica Mercado.

35. Few-Shot Parameter-Efficient Fine-Tuning is Better and Cheaper than In-Context Learning by Haokun Liu, Derek Tam, et al.

36. Parameter-Efficient Fine-Tuning without Introducing New Latency by Baohao Liao, Yan Meng, and Christof Monz.

37. LoRA: Low-Rank Adaptation of Large Language Models by Edward J. Hu, Yelong Shen, et al.

38. AI Now Institute: The Climate Costs of Big Tech.

39. Making AI Less "Thirsty": Uncovering and Addressing the Secret Water Footprint of AI Models by Pengfei Li, Jianyi Yang, et al.

40. Model Cards for Model Reporting by Margaret Mitchell, et al.

41. Datasheets for Datasets by Timnit Gebru, et al.

42. Prompt Programming for Large Language Models: Beyond the Few-Shot Paradigm by Laria Reynolds and Kyle McDonell.

43. Chain-of-Thought Prompting Elicits Reasoning in Large Language Models by Jason Wei, Xuezhi Wang, et al.

44. Unified Scaling Laws for Routed Language Models by Aidan Clark, Diego de las Casas, et al.

45. Calibration of Pre-trained Transformers by Shrey Desai and Greg Durrett.

46. Anthropic: Constitutional AI: Harmlessness from AI Feedback by Yuntao Bai, Saurav Kadavath, et al.

47. Scalable agent alignment via reward modeling: a research direction by Jan Leike, David Krueger, et al.

47. Open AI: Deep reinforcement learning from human preferences by Paul Christiano, Jan Leike, et al.

48. Intermediate-Task Transfer Learning with Pretrained Models for Natural Language Understanding: When and Why Does It Work? by Yada Pruksachatkun, Jason Phang, et al.

49 Hugging Face: Parameter-Efficient Fine-Tuning (PEFT)

50. Microsoft: LORA: Low-Rank Adaptation of Large Language Models by Edward Hu, Yelong Shen, et al.

51. Multitask Prompted Training Enables Zero-Shot Task Generalization by Victor Sanh, Albert Webson, et al.

52. OpenAI: Learning to summarize from human feedback by Nisan Stiennon, Long Ouyang, et al.

53. ReAct: Synergizing Reasoning and Acting in Language Models by Shunyu Yao, Jeffrey Zhao, et al.

54. Distributed AI Research Institute (DAIR)

55. Vice: OpenAI Used Kenyan Workers Making $2 an Hour to Filter Traumatic Content from ChatGPT by Chloe Xiang

56. FactSheets: Increasing Trust in AI Services through Supplier's Declarations of Conformity by Matthew Arnold, Rachel K. E. Bellamy, et al.

57. Data Statements for Natural Language Processing: Toward Mitigating System Bias and Enabling Better Science by Emily M. Bender and Batya Friedman.

58. Nutritional Labels for Data and Models by Julia Stoyanovich and Bill Howe.

59. The Dataset Nutrition Label: A Framework to Drive Higher Data Quality Standards by Sarah Holland, Ahmed Hosny, et al.

60. The Data Nutrition Project by Kasia Chmielinski, et al.

61. Google: Switch Transformers: Scaling to Trillion Parameter Models with Simple and Efficient Sparsity by William Fedus, Barret Zoph, and Noam Shazeer.

62. GLaM: Efficient Scaling of Language Models with Mixture-of-Experts by Nan Du, Yanping Huang, et al.

63. Google: BERT: Pre-training of Deep Bidirectional Transformers for Language Understanding by Jacob Devlin, Ming-Wei Chang, Kenton Lee, and Kristina Toutanova.

64. Open (For Business): Big Tech, Concentrated Power, and the Political Economy of Open AI by David Gray Widder, Sarah West, and Meredith Whittaker.

65. Yuening Jia, CC BY-SA 3.0, via Wikimedia Commons.

66. ChatGPT, Public domain, via Wikimedia Commons.

67. Marxav, CC0, via Wikimedia Commons.

68. Singerep, CC BY-SA 4.0, via Wikimedia Commons.

69. Holistic Evaluation of Language Models by Percy Liang, Rishi Bommasani, et al.

70. Measuring Massive Multitask Language Understanding by Dan Hendrycks, Collin Burns, et al.

71. Beyond the Imitation Game: Quantifying and extrapolating the capabilities of language models by Aarohi Srivastava, Abhinav Rastogi, et al.

72. GLUE: A multi-task benchmark and analysis platform for natural language understanding by Alex Wang, Amanpreet Singh, et al.

73. SuperGLUE: A Stickier Benchmark for General-Purpose Language Understanding Systems by Alex Wang, Yada Pruk-sachatkun, Nikita Nangia, et al.

Made in United States
Orlando, FL
25 June 2024

48295454R00137